Architect's Poc
Modern Mana
Practice

CW00921552

This book is an easily digestible guide to the management and practice knowledge needed to establish and run an architectural practice. It is of particular interest to those starting out in the profession and to students, whilst also being useful to architects more widely who need succinct information to assist them in the daily management of their work. The book sits beside the *Architect's Legal Pocket Book* providing legal information and the *Architect's Pocket Book* providing guidance in design. It covers all the main management and practice topics relevant to the running of an architectural business including setting up the company, the profession, project management, fees, office management, financial management and teamwork. It also looks at the state of the construction industry and the architectural profession today, new forms of practice, and how the profession is changing. The book is interweaved with pearls of wisdom and experience and reflections from architects, bringing the topics to life and aiding the reader's understanding.

Ben Vickery is an architect with more than 35 years' experience in architecture as a practice principal and as a designer and manager of projects, including high-profile major buildings in England and around the world. He runs his own practice, Vickery Hyett Sports Architecture, alongside which he teaches management at the University of Hertfordshire school of architecture.

Architect's Pocket Book of Modern Management and Practice

Ben Vickery

Routledge
Taylor & Francis Group

LONDON AND NEW YORK

First published 2025
by Routledge
4 Park Square, Milton Park, Abingdon, Oxon OX14 4RN

and by Routledge
605 Third Avenue, New York, NY 10158

Routledge is an imprint of the Taylor & Francis Group, an informa business

British Library Cataloguing-in-Publication Data
A catalogue record for this book is available from the British Library

Library of Congress Cataloging-in-Publication Data
Names: Vickery, Ben, author.
Title: The architect's pocket book of modern management and practice / Ben Vickery.
Description: Abingdon, Oxon ; New York, NY : Routledge, 2025. | Includes bibliographical references and index.
Identifiers: LCCN 2024037050 (print) | LCCN 2024037051 (ebook) | ISBN 9781032355283 (hardback) | ISBN 9781032355276 (paperback) | ISBN 9781003327288 (ebook)
Subjects: LCSH: Architectural practice—Great Britain—Management—Handbooks, manuals, etc.
Classification: LCC NA1996 .V53 2025 (print) | LCC NA1996 (ebook) | DDC 720.23/41—dc23/eng/20240919
LC record available at https://lccn.loc.gov/2024037050
LC ebook record available at https://lccn.loc.gov/2024037051

ISBN: 9781032355283 (hbk)
ISBN: 9781032355276 (pbk)
ISBN: 9781003327288 (ebk)

DOI: 10.4324/9781003327288

Typeset in Frutiger
by Apex CoVantage, LLC

To Susan and Sophie

Contents

Acknowledgements   *xi*

List of acronyms   *xiii*

Definitions   *xv*

1 Introduction   **1**

**Introduction to the construction industry
and the architectural profession**   **3**

2 The construction industry   **5**
Introduction   5
The Latham report   5
The Egan report   6
CDM   7
Modern methods of construction (MMC)   7
The Grenfell Tower tragedy   8
The Hackitt report   8
The Morrell report   10
The Building Safety Act 2022   10
The diversity of the construction industry   11
Design-and-build (D&B)   12
Developing trends   12

3 The architectural profession   **15**
The architect   15
The RIBA and ARB   16
Forms of practice   19

Practice management   **25**

4 Setting up a practice   **27**
Introduction   27
Pre-conditions   28
The business plan   28
The structure of the practice   31

	Insurance	38
	The practice name	40
	Accounts	41
5	**Marketing and business development**	**43**
	Introduction	43
	Planning marketing and business development	46
	Keeping in touch	47
	Costs	53
	Review of the marketing and business development plan	53
	Winning a project	54
6	**People management**	**59**
	Introduction	59
	Hiring	60
	The employment contract	63
	Managing people	67
	Leadership	70
7	**Finances**	**75**
	Introduction	75
	The practice finances	76
	Project finances	86
	Competitive tendering	92
	VAT	92
	Inflation	94
	Invoicing	94
	Sub-consultants	96
	Ongoing project cost control	96
8	**Environmental sustainability**	**99**
	Introduction	99
	The environmental sustainability policy	99
	Communications	100
	The sustainable office	100
	Environmental sustainability of projects	101

Project management   **107**

9 Project delivery   **109**
Introduction   109
The RIBA Plan of Work   109
The architect's appointment   113
General principles of project communications   119
Project meetings   119
Project set-up   121
The RIBA Plan of Work stages   131

10 Planning   **161**
Introduction   161
Planning in England   162
Planning in Scotland   170
Planning in Wales   171
Planning in Northern Ireland   171
Historic buildings   172

11 Building control and CDM   **175**
Introduction   175
The Building Regulations   175
The process of building control   179
The Building Regulations application and approval
  process in England and Wales   181
The Building Safety Act 2022   182
The building standards application and approval
  process in Scotland   184
The Building Regulations application and approval
  process in Northern Ireland   185
Construction health and safety (CDM)   185

12 Building contracts   **187**
Introduction   187
Traditional contracts   188
Design-and-build contracts   189
Management contracts   192
Which contract type?   195

The contract form 198
Managing a construction contract 201

13 Quality assurance **211**
Introduction 211
The office manual and office quality manual 212
Quality management systems (QMS) 215

14 Computing **217**
Introduction 217
Hardware 217
Storage and backup 218
Production systems 220
Management and accounts systems 226

Bibliography *231*

Index *235*

Acknowledgements

The author would like to thank the people who have assisted with the writing of this book including his colleagues at Vickery Hyett architects, Paul Hyett, Jamie Hay and Jacob Steele; Francis Henderson for his broad knowledge of management; Chris Annis FCA at LB Group Chartered Accountants for assistance with the financial chapter; Konrad Frankowski for input on computing matters; Mark Lucas for reading and commenting on the text; Stephen Barnshaw for assistance with building control matters; Adrain Dobson at the RIBA for suggestions, and Geraint John for proposing the subject of the book in the first place.

Acronyms

AI	Artificial Intelligence
ARB	The Architects Registration Board
BIM	Building Information Modelling
BRE	The Building Research Establishment
BREEAM	Building Research Establishment Environmental Assessment Method
BSI	The British Standards Institution
BSR	The Building Safety Regulator established by the Building Safety Act
CA	Contract Administrator, a defined term in the standard JCT construction contract
CDM	Construction Design and Management
CPD	Continuing Professional Development
GDPR	General Data Protection Regulations
HMRC	His Majesty's Revenue and Customs
HR	Human Resources
HRB	Higher Risk Building. Defined in the Building Safety Act
HSE	The Health and Safety Executive
IT	Information Technology
JCT	The Joint Contracts Tribunal
LABC	Local Authority Building Control
LEED	Leadership in Energy and Environmental Design
LLP	Limited Liability Partnership
MMC	Modern Methods of Construction
NBS	The National Building Specification
NPPF	The National Planning Policy Framework
PII	Professional Indemnity Insurance
QA	Quality Assurance
QMS	Quality Management System
QS	Quantity Surveyor, a building cost consultant
RIBA	The Royal Institute of British Architects
RIAS	The Royal Institute of Architects in Scotland

SBC 2016	The Standard Building Contract 2016 edition, published by the JCT
VAT	Value-Added Tax
VR	Virtual Reality

Definitions

Cost plan: Building Cost Plan and Project Cost Plan

Building cost plan

The cost of the construction of a building normally including a contractor's overhead and profit.

Project cost plan

The cost of a building project including the cost of construction of the building plus all the other costs necessary to get it designed, built and occupied – land purchase, consultants' fees, client's management costs, financing costs, planning fees and costs, sales costs and the like.

Both of the aforementioned are prepared by the quantity surveyor or cost consultant to identify the cost of the building or project. They should not be confused with the building or project budget – that is the figure, normally set by the client, of the amount they want to spend. The project cost plan needs to fit within the project budget.

Architects might also refer to their own internal cost plan for a project as a 'project cost plan'. This refers to the architectural practice's own cost of staff, project expenses and office overheads to carry out a project.

1
Introduction

An architect's core competency is designing buildings, but in order to get their designs built and to run a practice they also need to be competent in management. There is much knowledge to acquire and many skills to learn to manage a project and a practice. The author intends that readers should become competent in the management aspect of their profession and even enjoy it.

This book is written as an easily digestible, 'user-friendly' guide to setting up and running an architectural practice and architectural projects in the United Kingdom. As such, it covers all the primary aspects of practice management and project delivery, leaving design, and the design process, to many other sources. It is based on the knowledge and experience of the author reinforced by input from various specialists.

It is intended to be of particular interest to those starting out in practice and to students, whilst also being useful to all those architects who need succinct information and guidance to assist them in the daily management of their work. It therefore includes useful information in an easily accessible format to assist architects with the daily management of their work and to give advice based on experience where possible.

The reader should note that much of the information from external sources mentioned in the text changes regularly, notably regulations and company and product information, but also other government and commercial information and guidance. The reader should always check the original source information to confirm it.

DOI: 10.4324/9781003327288-1

References to books and other sources are offered throughout the text which will assist the reader where further information and guidance are required. The legal background to liability, company forms and other aspects of architects' work is not explained here as it can be found in other texts referred to in the bibliography.

This *Architect's Pocket Book of Modern Management and Practice* sits alongside the *Architect's Legal Pocket Book* [1] and the *Building Regulations Pocket Book* [2] to which reference is made throughout the text.

References

[1]   Cousins, N. 2020. *Architect's Legal Pocket Book*. Abingdon and Oxfordshire: Routledge.
[2]   Tricker, R. and Alford, S. 2023. *Building Regulations Pocket Book*. Abingdon and Oxfordshire: Routledge.

Introduction to the construction industry and the architectural profession

2
The construction industry

Introduction

In this chapter we make some observations and comments about the construction industry in 2024. The construction industry is approximately 10% of Britain's gross domestic product (GDP) as reported in the Egan Report [2], some of which is public sector work, therefore the government has taken an interest not only in planning, building regulations and site safety but also in improving the industry's efficiency and quality of output.

The Latham report

In 1994 the government commissioned a report from Sir Michael Latham [1] called 'Constructing the Team' that criticised the UK construction industry as 'ineffective', 'adversarial', 'fragmented' and 'incapable of delivering for its customers'. This fits with the author's own experience of construction projects in the period when a few contractors tried to make profits by offering a low tender then making claims for additional money from the first day on site. The report recommended 'partnering', which included the concept of teamwork between supplier and client, in a process of total continuous improvement. Such a process would require openness between the parties, acceptance of new ideas, trust and perceived mutual benefit. There were a series of specific recommendations, however the Labour government commissioned another report in 1997.

DOI: 10.4324/9781003327288-3

The Egan report

The *Report of the Construction Task Force*, the 'Egan report' [2] authored by Sir John Egan, former chairman of Jaguar Cars, said it was written in light of a view that the UK construction industry was underachieving and was informed by experience from other sectors. The report recommended change driven by committed leadership, a focus on the customer, integrated processes and teams, a quality-driven agenda and commitment to people. A target was set of a 10% annual reduction in construction costs and construction time accompanied by a 20% annual reduction in construction defects. It said this would involve integrated processes around product development, project implementation, partnering the supply chain and production of components. Specifically, it recommended replacing competitive tendering with long-term relationships based around the open measurement of performance.

The report also recommended a change in culture to provide decent and safe working conditions and improve management and supervisory skills at all levels.

Various initiatives resulted from the Egan report to coordinate best practice and innovation throughout the industry. These continue today under the auspices of Constructing Excellence (www.constructingexcellence.org.uk) part of the BRE group of companies. The Strategic Forum for Construction, set up by the government in 2001 under Sir John Egan, published a report titled *Accelerating Change* in 2002 [3]. This underlined the importance of developing information technology and set the tone for the government drive from 2010 onwards under its chief construction adviser, Paul Morrell, to implement BIM on all public sector construction projects.

Although there may be more partnering and long-term relationships in the construction industry than there were before Egan, it is the author's experience that competitive tendering is still common.

CDM

The safety of workers on building sites has improved in recent years following the publication in 1994 of European Directive 92/57/EEC on minimum safety and health standards on construction sites across the Union, the current UK regulations for which are the Construction (Design and Management) Regulations (CDM Regulations) 2015. This is described in Chapter 11 Building control and CDM.

Modern methods of construction (MMC)

A National Audit Office (NAO) report in 2005 [4] suggested MMC including:

- Construction of three-dimensional modular units in a factory to be assembled on site into a larger building;
- Panellised units produced in a factory and assembled on site into a three-dimensional structure;
- Hybrid techniques combining panellised and volumetric approaches;
- Other factory production of elements or assemblies such as roof or floor cassettes, pre-cast foundation assemblies, pre-formed wiring looms, and certain innovative techniques such as tunnel form or thin-joint blockwork.

The NAO report was written to encourage the construction of more homes in less time with less on-site labour.

Such techniques have existed since, for example, the construction of prefabricated homes during and after the Second World War. They were given encouragement when in the Autumn Budget of 2017 the government suggested it would favour MMC for public infrastructure projects from 2019 and they now seem to be gaining more prominence in the industry.

The Grenfell Tower tragedy

The Grenfell Tower tragedy in June 2017 showed all parts of the construction industry to have performed poorly on the project of renovation of the residential block that led to the fatal fire. It was brought into public view at the Inquiry set up to 'examine the circumstances leading up to and surrounding the fire' [5] that all the main parties involved in the refurbishment of the 24-storey tower did not pay enough attention to the fire safety aspects of their work, resulting in an unsafe building. Following the tragedy and before the completion of the Inquiry, the government has introduced a range of measures that affect most aspects of the industry. The Phase 3 report of the Inquiry into the tragedy will be published in 2024 setting out the recommendations for future action proposed by the advisers to the Inquiry. These may persuade the government to make further changes, however further legislation or guidance has yet to be published at the time of writing.

The Hackitt report

As part of the government's response to the Grenfell Tower tragedy, Dame Judith Hackitt was commissioned in 2018 to write an *Independent Review of Building Regulations and Fire Safety* [6]. In the report she stated, 'the regulatory system covering high-rise and complex buildings was not fit for purpose'. She recommended therefore the establishment of a new regulatory framework for buildings ten storeys high or more including:

- A new joint regulatory authority (which she called the JCA) comprising Local Authority Building Control (LABC), fire brigades and HSE to oversee safety throughout the life of the buildings;
- A mandatory incident reporting system for fires and other buildings safety failures that should allow them to be reported on a no-blame basis;

- During the construction phase new dutyholder responsibilities modelled on those in the CDM regulations;
- A series of robust gateway points through the design and construction processes to strengthen regulatory oversight;
- A stronger change control process for amendments to a design during regulatory approval and construction;
- A 'golden thread' of information on the safety of buildings (called the Fire and Emergency File, FEF) to be held in digital format;
- Oversight of HRBs occurring only through the JCA with LABC and approved inspectors assisting;
- More rigorous enforcement powers;
- The JCA should have oversight throughout the life of the building.

This stronger regime of regulatory oversight during the life of a high-rise residential building when it is occupied should include a new dutyholder with a requirement to present a safety case to the JCA at intervals. This regime should apply to new buildings and to existing ones, though for the latter the requirements may be less. Clearer rights and obligations for residents of the buildings were proposed including obligations to be part of the maintenance of the safety of the buildings.

Hackitt suggested that Building Regulations should emphasise fire safety as a system, not individual components, and also that a more robust and transparent products testing and certification regime should be developed. She recommended the creation of a new Approved Document to describe all the safety systems of a high-rise residential building. She recommended the competence of those involved with safety design of buildings should be improved, including architects. Poor procurement practices should be tackled and building contracts should be arranged so that safety is not compromised.

The Morrell report

In parallel with Hackitt's report Paul Morrell was commissioned to look at the regime for the testing and certification of construction products [7]. The primary construction product regulation is the EU Construction Products Regulation (EU CPR305/11) brought into UK law in 2011 and updated by Construction Products Regulations 2013, identified by the CE mark. Morrell recommended changes to the regime of product certification, none of which have been implemented at the time of writing.

The Building Safety Act 2022

The government has implemented the majority of Hackitt's recommendations set out in her report through the Building Safety Act [8]. Some of the primary parts of the Act are:

- The establishment of a new Building Safety Regulator (BSR) underneath the Health and Safety Executive to oversee building control approvers and inspectors, and to carry out the building control function for a new category of 'Higher Risk Buildings' (HRBs), primarily high-rise housing, also care homes and hospitals.
- A new building approval process for Higher Risk Buildings involving three 'gateways'; the first at planning submission stage, the second a Building Regulations approval before start on site and the third at completion of construction. Each of these gateways must be passed before a project can move on to the next, so at gateway two Building Regulations approval must be received before construction can commence, and at gateway three a Completion Certificate must be received before a building can be occupied. For Higher Risk Buildings there is also a new requirement to apply for Building Regulations approval for changes to the design occurring after the issue of the gateway two approval, which may be during the construction phase.

Construction cannot commence on the changed design until approval is received.
- The creation of new dutyholders during construction and occupation of HRBs.
- All HRBs must be registered with the BSR and when occupied the dutyholder must carry out a safety case report to be submitted to the BSR, which must be updated at intervals.

In addition to this the government has implemented amendments to the Building Regulations and the recommendations of the Approved Documents including increased restrictions on the use of combustible materials in external walls, the requirement for two staircases in taller residential buildings and other changes.

These new processes are an additional administrative burden for the construction and operation of the buildings covered by the act, the effect of which has yet to work its way through the industry.

The diversity of the construction industry

Contractors and builders operating in Britain range in size from individuals carrying out a trade on small projects or as sub-contractors on larger projects to multinational contractors, and many sizes in between. They are each capable of different work on projects and the architect, if asked to assist the client in this way, must find the appropriate building contracting organisation for any task.

The small builder working on individual houses will typically work under a traditional contract and will not have financial resources to cope with being paid long in arrears. Large contractors may have greater resources and some have the ability to act as a developer in the financing of construction projects. In the area of new-build housing many developers carry out their own construction. Some of the larger companies in the construction sector focus entirely on management with all the actual construction on the sites they manage carried out by sub-contractors.

Design-and-build (D&B)

Currently 'design-and-build' is a common method for delivery of projects throughout the construction industry. It is used for many building types from hospitals or other large buildings through to single houses. As a delivery method it has advantages, notably that a client has a single point of contact for the design and construction of their project, and it can enable projects to be delivered quickly and perhaps at a lower cost. It has however attracted criticism as a result of the Grenfell fire where the refurbishment of the tower was delivered through a design-and-build contract. Although the full implications of the new regulatory regime from the Building Safety Act have not worked their way through the industry yet, it is likely to be more difficult to deliver projects through design-and-build contracts under the new processes.

Developing trends

The previous paragraphs discuss some of the topics influencing change in the UK construction industry at the time of writing. The author gives some other thoughts here about trends currently visible.

Given the UK's commitment to reduce energy consumption and to reduce degradation of the environment the construction of buildings must change. Some examples of this change visible at the moment are:

- the increasing use of more environmentally sustainable building materials, such as timber;
- the movement to build housing at higher densities in order to use less land area; and

- the movement to refurbish or reuse existing buildings wherever possible rather than building new.

How the new fire safety requirements mentioned earlier will be reconciled with timber construction is yet to be resolved.

Modern methods of construction, mentioned previously, are being used more widely whereby more construction work takes place in a factory and less on site. These are bringing new problems, as do all new methods of construction, however their advantages are such that they appear to be increasingly adopted. With them are new methods of delivery, such as the rental of mechanical and electrical equipment in place of its purchase for installation in buildings.

References

[1] Latham, M. 1994. *Constructing the Team*. London: HMSO.
[2] Egan, J. 1998. *Rethinking Construction: Report of the Construction Task Force*. London: HMSO.
[3] Egan, J. 2002. *Accelerating Change: Consultation Paper by Strategic Forum for Construction*. London: HMSO.
[4] National Audit Office Report. 2005. Using Modern Methods of Construction to Build Homes More Quickly and Efficiently. https://www.nao.org.uk/uploads/2005/11/mmc.pdf
[5] The Grenfell Tower Inquiry. https://grenfelltowerinquiry.org.uk
[6] Hackitt, D. J. 2018. *Building a Safer Future, Independent Review of Building Regulations and Fire Safety: Final Report*. London: HMSO.
[7] Morrell, P. and Day, A. 2023. *Testing for a Safer Future, An Independent Review of the Construction Products Testing Regime*. London: DLUHC.
[8] The Building Safety Act 2022. https://www.legislation.go.uk/ukpga/2022/30/contents/enacted

3
The architectural profession

The architect

Architects in the United Kingdom have normally completed seven years of education and training, have passed the RIBA parts I, II and III exams, are registered with the ARB and may be a member of the RIBA, so they have knowledge, skills and professional registration to prove it. By practising and completing Continuing Professional Development (CPD) they ensure their knowledge keeps up to date and they become experienced. It is this knowledge, skill and experience they are selling.

Barrington Kaye [1] defines a professional firstly as a person who holds special knowledge. He then identifies that professions have associations or other controlling bodies that regulate the education of their members to ensure they all have a certain standard of qualification. The associations also set standards of behaviour to ensure the integrity of the professionals, keep a register of their members and possibly also govern the fees they can charge. This arrangement works in the interest of the professionals as it ensures that only people whose work is of a controlled standard will be allowed to call themselves professionals. It also works in the interest of the public buying their services as they can rely on a certain quality of work and standard of behaviour.

The architect acts as the agent for his or her client in the design and construction of a building. The client needs to be able to trust their architect, which they can do partly because, as a member of the professional body, they know the architect has a certain level of qualifications and has signed up to the rules of behaviour of the body. The public's trust in the profession is

DOI: 10.4324/9781003327288-4

therefore protected at the national level by the RIBA and ARB, and at the project level by every architect's own actions.

The architect acts in the interest of his or her client. He or she also needs to act in the interest of those who will use the buildings they design, of the public who will live around those buildings and of wider society. All of this involves an altruistic, honest attitude and a correct regard for the many interests that exist related to any particular project and the environment more generally.

Architecture is identified as a profession in the United Kingdom. Architects are required by law to be registered with the Architects' Registration Board, to have completed their full architectural education and to hold professional indemnity insurance. They can also be a member of the Royal Institute of British Architects, or the institutes in Scotland, Wales and Northern Ireland which manage education and promote architecture in the public realm.

The RIBA and ARB

The first meeting of the Institute of British Architects was on 15 June 1835, and the institute was granted a royal charter in 1837. It had elected members and a code of conduct, but no 'measurers' (surveyors) were allowed or anyone connected to the building trades as they were seen as potentially open to corruption. At a General Conference of Architects in 1887 a proposal was adopted to establish three levels of exams, the foundation of the RIBA qualifications that exist today. The Institute of Architects of Scotland was founded in 1840 and granted a royal charter in 1916 to become the current Royal Incorporation of Architects in Scotland (RIAS). The Royal Institute of the Architects of Ireland (RIAI) was founded in 1840 to act for architects in Ireland. The Royal Society of Ulster Architects (RSUA) acts for architects in Northern Ireland and the Royal Society of Architects in Wales represents the profession in Wales.

The history of the ARB is somewhat different as this followed a campaign calling for legal registration of architects after which the Architects (Registration) Act 1931 was passed setting up the Architects Registration Council of the UK (ARCUK) with three committees: a Board of Architectural Education, an Admissions Committee and a Discipline Committee, creating confusion between its role and that of the RIBA from the start. The Act first enacted voluntary registration, then the Architects (Registration) Act 1938 enacted compulsory registration to use the name 'architect'.

The Architects Act 1997 dissolved ARCUK and replaced it with the Architects Registration Board (ARB) to manage the register of architects. The board of the ARB are appointed by the Privy Council with six of the 11 members including the chairperson required to be not registered architects. The ARB describes its role (arb.org.uk) as 'To ensure only those who are suitably competent are allowed to practise as architects' by approving qualifications, managing a register and setting standards of conduct and practice.

The RIBA describes itself [2] as 'a global professional membership body driving excellence in architecture. We serve our members and society in order to deliver better buildings and places'. The RIBA president and council are elected by its members.

The RIBA leads the profession by

- running the validation of courses at architecture schools in the United Kingdom and those abroad that wish for their qualifications to be recognised to offer the RIBA parts I, II and III;
- running CPD for their members;
- keeping a listing of member architects and practices and promoting them;
- managing information through the drawings collection and library;
- talking to government on behalf of the profession;

- publishing books and magazines about architecture;
- promoting architecture through initiatives such as annual architectural awards.

Architects around the world can also become members of the RIBA, though this membership does not give the person holding it the right to practise in the UK. Schools of architecture in many countries around the world have courses validated by the RIBA to give part I or II exemption.

When the UK was a member of the European Union, architects qualified in other EU countries gained the automatic right to registration in the UK. This was ended by the Architects Act 1997 (Amendment) Regulations 2023 and the ARB was enabled to seek mutual recognition with other bodies around the world.

To register with the ARB, and to become a member of the RIBA, students must complete three parts of their architectural education:

(1) A recognised part 1 qualification. This is a degree or equivalent.
(2) A recognised part 2 qualification. This is a post-graduate diploma, master's degree or equivalent.
(3) A recognised part 3 qualification. This is a professional practice qualification including exams and two years of work in an architect's office.

Continuing Professional Development

Architects are required to continually update their knowledge through a programme of annual learning. From January 2024 to remain on the register all architects are required to carry out CPD studies annually which can be recorded on the ARB's or the RIBA's website. The ARB stipulates two compulsory topics, fire and life safety and environmental sustainability, and the RIBA requires 35 hours a year of which half must be structured learning and half can be informal.

Insurance

To be on its register the ARB requires the architect to hold professional indemnity insurance (PII). This should be held either by the individual or by the company for which they work, if they are working for that company as an architect. If they are a registered architect but not practising, for example they may be a journalist, academic or researcher, they need not hold PII. For more information on PII see Chapter 4 Setting up a practice.

Forms of practice

We shall review here the main forms of architects' design practices. Although most architects work in design practices there are many working for other organisations, including larger engineering practices, developers, property owners who manage a large portfolio of buildings for example pubs and hotels, local government, government quangos and the like. We describe more detail of the legal structures of architectural practices including tax and other matters related to each practice organisation in Chapter 4 Setting up a practice.

The Architects Act 1997 allows architects to practise as sole traders, partnerships or limited liability partnerships or as companies, limited or unlimited. Generally there has been a move away from the forms of practice where liability is unlimited – sole traders and partnerships – towards those with limited liability – limited liability partnerships and limited companies.

Some practices are also moving towards a structure based around social purpose, including becoming registered charities, whilst others are acting as a developer as well as an architect.

• Sole trader

An individual carrying on business on their own account. Legally this is the simplest form of practice.

- Partnership

A partnership can be regarded as more than one sole trader working together, with or without a written agreement. This was traditionally the only form of practice permitted for architects, however the Architects Act 1997 permits registered persons to practise in the other arrangements described here. A key point is that the partners have a 'joint and several' liability so all partners are together liable for the work of the partnership irrespective of whether they were directly involved in the work. There are some exceptions to this, and the law is complicated, additionally a partnership does not require any formal registration and isn't obliged to make public certain information in the way that other entities do.

- Limited liability partnership (LLP)

This is a hybrid between a partnership and company whereby partners have limited liability. An LLP is a separate legal entity from its members and must be registered at Companies House.

- Limited liability company

A company is owned by its shareholders whose liability may be limited or unlimited. This is the most common form of practice for architects in the UK and for all sizes of company from architects working on their own to large international companies (RIBA Business Benchmarking 2022 report: [3]).

A company can be either a public limited company (commonly called a 'PLC') or a private limited company. A PLC's shares can be traded publicly and the company is therefore subject to additional regulations, whereas a private limited company will have a restrictive share agreement setting out that the shares can only change ownership by private agreement. Architecture companies are rarely public unless they are part of a larger organisation.

- Employee ownership

Many architects' practices have some form of employee ownership, as there is evidence that employees are more committed and motivated if they own a stake in the company. The share of ownership can be given as a reward for achievement or as a right when working in the company.

A limited liability company can transfer shares to its staff; the shares can be a gift, they can be sold to staff, or 'share options' can be given to the staff that allow them to buy shares in the future. Note that when the ownership of company equity is transferred the transaction may be subject to taxation.

Separate to their legal structure some practices are owned, or partially owned, by a trust set up to benefit the employees. A trust is a structure whereby assets are placed by the 'settlor' into the trust which is managed by 'trustees' on behalf of 'beneficiaries'. Architectural practices are either owned by Employee Ownership Trusts or Employee Benefit Trusts.

An Employee Ownership Trust (EOT), as defined by the Finance Act 2014, is a trust created to hold shares in a company on behalf of its employees, so that they become the owners indirectly. The trust need not own all the company's equity, but if it owns more than 50% then it can give bonuses up to £3,600 per year tax free (figure correct in 2024), noting the bonuses must be given to all employees on an equal basis. There are tax benefits for shareholders transferring their shares into the trust. An Employee Benefit Trust is a simpler mechanism whereby the trust holds shares in the name of the employees, but it is not an EOT as defined in the 2014 Act.

In recent years some practices have wanted to move towards more socially conscious arrangements in the company's internal set-up. Some are also working with charities, non-government organisations (NGOs) or community groups to create buildings for social needs or to satisfy environmental or community aims. We look here at some alternative practice structures.

- Co-operative

The International Co-operative Alliance (ICA, the global federation of co-operative enterprises) defines a co-op as the following: 'A co-operative is an autonomous association of persons united voluntarily to meet their common economic, social and cultural needs and aspirations through a jointly-owned and democratically controlled enterprise'. Co-operatives are incorporated as companies, with limited liability or not, in one of the forms described previously, or their legal form can be that of a financial 'society', club, trust or other – it is the articles of association that will describe the management of the company according to co-operative principles.

There are many different types of co-operatives in different sectors of the economy, and in architecture the form is likely to be a workers' co-operative where all the people in the practice share in the control and profits of the company. For more information see: www.uk.coop/advice and the International Cooperative Alliance on www.ica.coop.

- Community interest company (CIC)

Created by the Companies (Audit, Investigations and Community Enterprise) Act 2005, these are organisations that wish to pursue local interests, but which are not eligible for charity status. They are limited liability companies registered with Companies House and they must also pass a community interest test, administered by the CIC Regulator [4]. They have a compulsory 'asset lock' so that their assets can only be used for the benefit of the community and cannot be distributed to members of the company or investors.

- Charity

A charity with limited liability is called a charitable incorporated organisation (CIO), or Scottish charitable incorporated organisation (SCIO). Some charities are required under law to become an incorporated body if they are employing people or signing contracts and until recently this has been done by becoming a limited company so that the charity is regulated by the Registrar of Companies and the Charity Commission. The Charities Act 2011 created a new form, the charitable incorporated organisation, that is regulated only by the Charity Commission and has limited liability. In Scotland this is a Scottish charitable incorporated organisation regulated by the Office of the Scottish Charity Regulator. There is no equivalent arrangement in Northern Ireland. The CIO or SCIO must have a governing body and can also have members, all of whom are required to act as charity trustees. For more information on CIOs see the government website [5].

• B Corp

Companies can become certified B Corporations to demonstrate their commitment to progressive aims. The certification is managed by B-Lab, a not-for-profit organisation with affiliates around the world [6], and covers social and environmental topics, openness, and accountability to all stakeholders. To become certified a company must complete an impact assessment, adopt or amend its articles of association to follow the B Corp requirements and sign the B Corp Declaration.

References

[1] Kaye, B. 1960. *The Development of the Architectural Profession in Britain*. London: George Allen and Unwin Ltd.
[2] The Royal Institute of British Architects. https://www.architecture.com
[3] RIBA Business Benchmarking Report. https://www.architecture.com/knowledge-and-resources/resources-landing-page/business-benchmarking
[4] The Community Interest Company Regulator. https://www.gov.uk/government/organisations/office-of-the-regulator-of-community-interest-companies
[5] The Charity Commission Regulations for Charitable Incorporated Organisations. https://www.gov.uk/government/publications/charity-commission-regulations-charitable-incorporated-organisations.
[6] B Corporations. https://www.b-corporation.net

Practice management

4
Setting up a practice

Introduction

For many architects, both young and older, their ambition is to have their own practice, whether alone or with others. For many the culmination of this ambition is to work for themselves, for others they set up with friends they have met at university or at employment in an established company, others again buy into an existing practice. This chapter sets out to guide architects starting a new practice.

This chapter discusses the pre-conditions for starting a new practice; the choice of practice structure, which is also discussed in Chapter 3 The architectural profession; insurance; the practice name, and finances, which are elaborated further in Chapter 7 Finances. The new practice will also need to get going with marketing and business development, discussed in Chapter 5 Marketing and business development; if it is hiring a team, it will need to start some people management, discussed in Chapter 6, and it will need to purchase software, discussed in Chapter 14 Computing.

If anyone intending to start up a practice is unsure about the company set-up, property ownership or similar legal issues, they are advised to seek legal advice. Solicitors can be found through the website of the Law Society [1], the Law Society of Scotland [2] and the Law Society of Ireland [3]. Financial advice and sometimes strategic advice about companies can be obtained from accountants – see later on finding a chartered accountant.

DOI: 10.4324/9781003327288-6

Pre-conditions

The first pre-condition for setting up a new practice is either an existing flow of work or some start-up working capital. Setting up a business costs money – to legally establish the company (if that is the structure decided on), to develop marketing material, to carry out business development and to pay accountants, lawyers and other advisors. The aspiring architect may be able to avoid some costs by carrying out much of the initial work of setting up the practice themselves, either way they should establish the likely cost of setting up before starting the process of doing so.

A cash reserve will also be needed to pay the principals and any employees to win and carry out work before money arrives in payment for that work. If the new practice carries out paid design work, the shortest period for which it will have to finance itself is two months if the first invoice is issued at the end of the first month and the invoice requests payment in 30 days. If the practice has to win the job first and if the client pays more slowly than 30 days, it can be financing itself for six months or more before being paid. The first payment is often slow to arrive as contract and payment protocols are being established. Of course, payment can be requested earlier, for example as an up-front payment before starting work, and the first invoice can be issued earlier than the end of the first month requesting payment faster than 30 days, but such arrangements outside the normal protocols will be subject to negotiation with the client.

The business plan

To maximise the chance that the business will be successful, a business plan, including a company strategy and a financial plan, should be developed for the new venture. The business plan should cover:

(1) A strategic description of the proposed practice setting out
- its philosophy,
- its intended structure – the legal structure and the working structure of the team,
- the intended market,
- how it is going to win work and
- how it is going to do it – the team required including senior and junior people, the software required, the working protocols and relationships with other consultants needed to complete the projects,
- the team,
- premises,
- the timing of setting up, winning and completing work, then getting paid, and
- all other matters important to the structure and operation of the new company.

Writing these out will help to solidify the ideas and will enable them to be communicated to colleagues, advisers, banks and others.

(2) A financial plan showing for the first year or more including
- Expected income. Noting the gap in timing between issuing an invoice and being paid, cash should be shown arriving a minimum of one month after the billing date, or a longer period depending on your experience.
- Expected outgoings, including sub-consultants, employees, office rent, IT equipment and software, and general overheads.
- Insurance.
- Taxes (such as PAYE, corporation tax if a company, VAT).
- Other costs such as marketing, branding, banking, staff training.

The plan should cover at least a year, preferably as long as you can reliably predict events. Note that banks and financing companies will want to see a business plan, particularly if start-up loans or an overdraft are required, and they will have their own requirements of what they want to see in it, and over what period of time. See Chapter 7 Finances for a typical annual financial forecast.

The practice should establish a clear idea of what type of design work it wants to target – a building type, a locality, conservation work or similar – and how it is going to set about winning it. The structure of the practice should then be constructed around the intended work – people with appropriate qualifications and experience, offices in an appropriate location, marketing suited to the clients.

It is best to write these thoughts down in a straightforward fashion as the introduction to the business plan and test them in discussion with others who have experience, as they will be able to comment on the logic gaps in the ideas and suggest how to succeed in the aims.

If the architect is setting up with others it is important that they trust and respect each other. Everyone involved should be open about their existing commitments, debts, available capital, intentions for the practice and abilities. It is good when the business owners are not the same and have a spread of complementary skills. The principals will have to work together closely for the future, so they must be able to get on with each other.

In writing the business plan the prospective practice principals should be conservatively realistic about everything – the work they are actually likely to win, not the work they would like to win, and the costs of insurance, rent, staff, consultants and others, then they should leave a broad margin for costs overshooting and income undershooting. It is always better to have a conservative estimate of likely success and to exceed it than to estimate more income than is realistic and fall behind.

The structure of the practice

The differing business structures that exist in the United Kingdom are described next, and the architect intending to start a new company should choose the one that will best suit the proposed practice. There is no limitation on the type of structure that the architect can choose; the characteristics of each structure in terms of liability, ability to expand and other matters are described as follows. More detail on the legal aspects of companies can be found in the *Architect's Legal Handbook* [4], and some more information on this topic is in Chapter 3 The architectural profession.

(a) Sole trader

If an architect is working on their own they can do this as a sole trader, which is the simplest legal structure, however there is potentially no limitation on liability.

Legal structure
There is no legal registration (i.e. at Companies House) required to act as a sole trader. It is just the architect doing business on their own behalf. They do need to register with HMRC though and ensure they complete personal tax returns to declare any self-employment profits for tax purposes. The sole trader can employ people.

Liability
The individual is responsible for all the debts and obligations he or she incurs with no limit on liability.

Tax
The sole trader will be taxed as an individual on their profits and subjected to income tax and national insurance.

(b) Partnership

Working with others in a partnership used to be the most common structure for architects, though practices are increasingly moving away from this due to the risk unlimited liability brings. Effectively a 'partnership' is a group of more than one 'sole trader'.

Legal structure

A partnership is a relationship between two or more individuals who carry out business together with a view to profit. A partnership can be created informally simply by working together, but it is better to have a written agreement between the partners.

A partnership should be defined by an agreement between the partners, though under the Partnership Act 1890 a partnership can be deemed to exist if architects work together on a series of projects even without a formal agreement. Such a partnership is not a legal entity, just the sum of the individuals in it. The partnership can employ people.

The partnership agreement should set out:

The name of the firm.
The place of business.
The start date and duration of the agreement.
Capital contributions by the partners, including what happens when a partner leaves or dies or the partnership is dissolved.
Property. What is owned by the partners as individuals and what is owned by the firm.
Rights and duties of the partners, covering work brought into the practice, holidays, sabbaticals, and so forth.
Profits and losses. How these are divided up.
Miscellaneous earnings. How income from writing, teaching or other activities outside the firm are to be dealt with.

Banking and accounts. Authority for expenditure, signing of accounts and the like.

Arrangements for retirement or death of partners, or dissolution of the partnership.

Restrictions on practice. Any arrangements to prevent partners competing with each other, whilst in the practice or upon leaving, including definitions of their areas of work.

Constitution of the firm, including provisions for changes to the constitution or to the organisation of the company.

Management of the partnership.

Restrictions on the practice, if any.

Insurances.

Settlement of disputes by arbitration or other means.

Constraints on partners leaving the practice, for example limitations on freedom to take clients, projects or staff, limitations on freedom to accept new work from past clients, limitations on rights to claim authorship of past projects carried out when in the practice.

Liability

The partners are jointly and severally responsible for the debts and obligations of the partnership, and therefore for those of the other partners individually, and there is no limit on their liability.

Tax

Just like for sole traders, the partnership will have to register with HMRC so that it can submit a partnership tax return, and then from this each partner will file their own personal tax return containing their share of the partnership profits, on which they will be taxed as an individual.

(c) Limited liability partnership (LLP)

These were introduced by the Limited Liability Partnership Act 2000 and are a hybrid between a company and a partnership.

Legal structure

The LLP is a legal entity that is registered at Companies House, the government organisation that incorporates and dissolves companies in the UK, registers their information and makes it available to the public. The LLP is set up with an agreement between the 'members' that form it, similar to that for a partnership, however the requirement to register at Companies House is similar to that for a limited liability company.

There is no requirement for an LLP to have any particular management structure. The membership agreement should cover arrangements for management and decision-making, capital contributions, distribution of profits, membership changes, dispute resolution, liquidation, termination, changes to the agreement and other matters as listed for such an agreement in the section on partnerships. Profits can be allocated to the members very flexibly, which is one of the main advantages of this structure.

The structure of a partnership or LLP suits a practice where each of the partners is winning and carrying out their own work, different from others where the work is won and carried out by the practice as a whole: this is a fundamental difference of philosophy and working method.

Liability

The LLP as an entity is responsible for its debts to the extent of its assets, and its members (there are no shareholders or directors) have limited liability.

Tax

LLPs are taxed similarly to partnerships.

(d) Private limited liability company

Most architectural practices in the UK (irrespective of their size) are private limited liability companies, most with a restrictive agreement so that shares may only be owned by employees of the company. A limited liability company's annual accounts are visible to the public at Companies House, and it must comply with the formalities set out in the Companies Act. They can be set up with a minimum of one person as a director, and at least one shareholder (who can be the director mentioned here too). It can be a flexible arrangement for doing business – shares can be issued to investors, new shareholders and so on as the company grows, and shares can be sold or given to new people when older shareholders want to hand the company on in a succession plan.

A company is a separate legal entity from its shareholders and directors and it may enter into contracts, employ staff, own property, be sued and be liable for debts separately from them. Only in rare cases can directors or shareholders be held liable for debts and obligations of the company, if the directors act fraudulently or allow a company to trade whilst in administration for example.

Legal structure

A limited liability company is a separate legal entity separate from its shareholders or officers. If it is sued the shareholders are liable to the face value of their shareholding, hence giving them 'limited liability', (subject to any personal guarantees of directors being in place). A limited liability company must be registered with Companies House to which it must provide documentation including:

- A memorandum of association setting out the object of the company. A template memorandum of association is available on the Companies House website [5].
- Articles of association containing the regulations of the company. (There are model articles that will apply by default if articles are not written specifically.) Standard articles of association, called 'model articles', are available on the Companies House website [6].

- The initial share capital of the company.
- Particulars of the directors and secretary. Companies must have at least one director, for whom an address must be given, which need not be their home address if they feel this might be a risk. A company secretary ensures that company follows corporate requirements and can facilitate communications at the board level. The name of the company secretary should be given if one is appointed.
- The registered address.

A company is normally managed by directors whose duties and remuneration are set out in the articles or agreed by shareholders. They must produce the annual report and accounts to be issued to Companies House and they have a duty to act with care and good faith in the interests of the company. Companies must hold regular management meetings and a shareholders' meeting at least once a year, all of which must be recorded.

Liability
The shareholders' liability is normally limited to the amount unpaid on the nominal value of the shares.

Tax
The company is taxed separately from its shareholders, officers and employees. Employees are paid a salary and shareholders can receive a dividend to share the distributable profits. Company profits are subject to corporation tax, and dividends attract an income tax cost, but at effective rates lower than 'normal' income tax rates charged against income.

(e) Public limited companies (PLC)

These are companies where the shares are traded publicly, and in the author's experience, they are not suited to architectural practices as the cost and additional complexities associated with public trading of the shares are too burdensome for their consultancy business. Some architects, however, work in PLCs where they are part of a larger organisation, such as a developer or contractor.

There is also a risk in the author's view that being part of a PLC generates a potentially serious conflict with the notion of being a 'professional'. Partly this arises from the fact that the architect may come under the influence of shareholders who have little understanding of the business and partly because the managing director or chief executive officer of such an operation may, in trying to satisfy shareholders expectations regarding profits, restrict the level of the service below that which would otherwise be expected of a professional, in terms of duties both to client and to the public.

Legal structure
This is similar to a private limited company, but the trading of shares publicly brings additional administrative and legal requirements, and therefore costs, risks and regulations.

(f) Community interest company

Companies House identifies community interest companies (CIC) as a special type of limited company which exists to benefit the community rather than private shareholders. These need to be approved by the Community Interest Company Regulator whilst otherwise having most of the elements of the legal structure of a limited company. They can be limited by shares or by guarantee whereby individuals agree to pay the debts of the company up to a fixed limit. CICs are required to have an 'asset lock' ensuring that the assets are used for the benefit of the community as intended. They must file to Companies House an annual report as any other company plus a CIC report setting out how their social objectives are being fulfilled, which will be reviewed by the CIC Regulator. Model constitutions are available from the government website [7].

(g) Co-operatives or charities

Architects can set themselves up as co-operatives, which are discussed in Chapter 3 The architectural profession. These will be established on the basis of one of the legal structures described earlier or by becoming a 'financial society', club or trust. The articles of association will describe the functioning of the organisation on co-operative principles.

If architects wish to establish themselves as a charity, they can do so either as a standard charity or as a charitable incorporated organisation with limited liability, both of which are regulated by the Charity Commission. Charities generally pay less tax than limited companies provided all the income is used for charitable purposes. More information can be found at the government website [8].

Insurance

Architects are legally required to be insured to carry out their work: firstly, they need professional indemnity insurance, and they should also hold employer's liability insurance, public liability insurance and others.

Professional indemnity insurance (PII)

Standard 8 of the ARB's Architects Code states:

> You are expected to have adequate and appropriate professional indemnity insurance cover for you, your practice and your employees. You should ensure that your insurance remains adequate to meet a claim. You are expected to maintain a minimum level of cover, including run-off cover, in accordance with ARB's guidance.

Professional indemnity insurance pays for losses and damage of third parties, not loss caused to the insured practice's own business, and normally will pay for legal costs in fighting claims. The policy will normally cover the architect for sums they will be liable to pay as a result of court orders, arbitration or settlements, whether resulting from a breach of contract or tort. The insurance pays out for claims against the architect resulting from their negligence (defined as failing to take due care) or incompetence (defined as lacking in knowledge, skill or experience). Breach of contract and tort are discussed more fully in the *Architect's Legal Pocket Book* and similar legal reference books.

The amount insured should be appropriate to the scale and value of the work being carried out and clients will often stipulate what they want, which request will be a subject of commercial discussion as part of the appointment. There will be an excess, the amount paid by the insured before the insurer starts to pay, and the policy will be structured as either, say, '£5 million for each and every claim' or '£5 million as an aggregate limit' for all claims in each year or linked in some other way, for example they all arise from the same originating cause.

Professional indemnity policies usually provide cover for claims made in the period of the insurance, not for design errors made in that period. The error leading to the claim may have been made many years ago and for this reason practitioners need to keep insurance running long after they have retired.

It is important to notify the practice's insurers as soon as a situation arises that might lead to a claim: for example, if a contractor is accusing the architect of making an error that is costing them money, and the architect sees that there is a problem there, they must notify their insurer. Whether the situation constitutes a claim or a circumstance that might give rise to a claim, the architect will have to judge, but the notification should be as early as possible as a failure to notify might give the insurer cause not to pay. This is particularly important around the time of the annual renewal if the insurer is changed.

Employer's liability insurance

Employers in the United Kingdom are required to hold insurance to compensate employees for injury or ill health resulting from their employment.

Public liability insurance

Owners or lessees of property may be liable for loss or injury caused to members of the public due to their negligence or that of their staff and should take out insurance against this.

Other insurance

Architects may also need to buy property insurance to cover loss or damage to property or contents, motor insurance, travel insurance, health care insurance, disaster recovery insurance to cover against the loss of documents and other information from IT failures or the like, and others depending on the specific nature of their business.

The practice name

Since the term 'architect' is protected under the Architects Act 1997, only those registered with the ARB may call themselves architects. After this most practices, if they don't call themselves after the names of the principals, have a name that represents the philosophy or market of the company. If a practice wishes to use the word 'architect' in their name, then a Rule 20 application should be made to the ARB who can issue a letter confirming their consent to this (which will be required by others, e.g. Companies House) if the architect intends to register a limited company or LLP.

The name should be checked against existing names of other practices and firms of every sort to ensure there is no similarity that could lead to confusion or conflict. It is also worth thinking about how the name will sound when said out loud, how it might be shortened as an acronym, and how it might work as a web domain name.

Accounts

The company's accounts will need to be started from day one of doing business, or in fact from when the process of setting up the business commences. Chapter 7 Finances talks about how the business accounts may be structured. Decisions will have to be made about the structure to use with regards to tax matters, commercial matters and cashflow or other matters.

The income and expenditure should be calculated each month, if not more frequently, and the financial plan updated at least every three months.

Value-added tax (VAT). Any organisation be it sole trader, partnership or limited company with 'vatable' income of more than £90,000 (figure correct as of 1 April 2024) is required to register with HMRC for VAT, meaning that it has to additionally charge value-added tax on its fees; it can then reclaim back the VAT it has paid on business items bought.

An accountant will be able to prepare and submit annual accounts, and they may also advise on tax or on bookkeeping – or do it themselves – and give more general financial and strategic advice. Firms range from individuals to large multinationals and a chartered accountant can be found through the website of the Institute of Chartered Accountants of England and Wales [9], the Institute of Chartered Accountants of Scotland [10] or, for Northern Ireland, Chartered Accountants Ireland [11].

References

[1] The Law Society. https://www.lawsociety.org.uk
[2] The Law Society of Scotland. https://www.lawscot.org.uk

[3] The Law Society of Ireland. https://www.lawsociety.ie

[4] Speaight, K. C. A. and Thorne, M. 2021. *Architect's Legal Handbook: The Law for Architects*. Abingdon and Oxfordshire: Routledge.

[5] Companies House, Template Memorandum of Association. https://www.gov.uk/government/collections/memorandum-of-association-templates-for-limited-companies

[6] Model Articles of Association for Limited Companies. https://www.gov.uk/guidance/model-articles-of-association-for-limited-companies

[7] Companies House, Community Interest Company Model Constitution. https://www.gov.uk/government/publications/community-interest-companies-consitutions

[8] Information on Setting Up a Charity. https://www.gov.uk/setting-up-charity

[9] The Institute of Chartered Accountants of England and Wales. www.icaew.com

[10] The Institute of Chartered Accountants of Scotland. www.icas.com

[11] Chartered Accountants Ireland. www.charteredaccountants.ie

5
Marketing and business development

Introduction

Marketing is the activity of getting the company name and 'brand' established and advertised to those who matter through the website, emails, cards and leaflets, advertising, and the like. It is the process of promotion; that is, ensuring the practice is known by the audiences that commission work or by those who assist and advise those who commission work.

Business development is the pursuit of projects through contacting potential clients and organisations who might commission work. It is the identification of markets, projects, clients or other collaborators (consultants you want to bid with) and securing the opportunity to be considered or shortlisted or to compete for the project. Business development is the successful securing of work opportunities, and relationships with clients and consultants, that one identifies for pursuit.

We have described in preceding chapters that a practice should have a target market, and a practice character or philosophy. An architectural company, and particularly a new practice, is more likely to be successful if it targets a particular type of building, connection to a site or locality, has a clear design philosophy or specialises in a particular area. In the author's view the architectural market is crowded, so potential clients will find it easier to identify the company they want for their project if they can see one that specialises in that type of work. They are more likely to have confidence in the practice if they can see experience or specialist knowledge in the type of building they want to build.

DOI: 10.4324/9781003327288-7

Most clients want their project delivered efficiently to the highest quality within their allocated budget, which means delivering the best value for money with the fewest problems, both during design and construction and after completion. To achieve this they are likely to choose a practice that has designed similar buildings before and whose buildings have been a notable success. They want an architect with the technical knowledge of their type of building and with the design skills to achieve the results that matter to them – whether this is a beautiful home or a commercial building that makes the maximum profit. They will also want someone who knows how to navigate the various approvals and other bureaucratic processes along the way of the project, so again experience will count in this. Most importantly, most clients want to be sure their building will be constructed with the minimum of fuss, on time and on budget with competent quality management that will ensure a reliable, fault-free product. The level of fees will also influence clients' choice of architect. We discuss fees in Chapter 7 Finances. In summary, setting aside the aesthetic aspects of design, the three principal issues are, not necessarily in order of importance:

- technical competence in design, in detailing and on site;
- management of projects to deliver them successfully on time and with the minimum of fuss;
- the level of fees.

A company that specialises in large commercial buildings may struggle to complete a small house extension successfully and profitably: the skills needed for these types of buildings are different and the company needs to be organised differently to carry out these dissimilar types of work. The staff in the first company will come to have in-depth knowledge of the design and management of their commercial projects, where the issues involved in conception and implementation are not the same as those for the house extension. The company may have human resources, accounts, technical support staff and other overheads refined to support the efficient delivery of large commercial buildings, but are wholly unsuited to client relations and profitability on a much smaller scale project. This is not a hard and fast rule, but is part of the picture of increasing specialisation in architectural practice that we are seeing.

Furthermore, many clients will want to know their architect personally, particularly for smaller projects, that they can trust him or her and that he or she will be able to have a good working relationship with them for the time it will take to deliver their project, which, in the case of most building types, is a matter of years.

So once the character of the practice has been established, what are the routes to winning work? In order to clarify how to achieve the practice you are striving for, draft a description of what you want your practice to be, and then write a plan of how to get there – a marketing and business development plan. The following are the primary methods to getting a company known and meeting potential clients, noting that the right marketing and business development plan will be different for each building type or market sector.

Firstly, people will be willing to employ an architect to carry out their project if they know them, so personal contact is the primary route to winning projects. To know the people who commission the type of work the practice is seeking to be involved with, the architect will need to find out where those people spend time, what work events they attend such as conferences and social gatherings or how otherwise they might want to meet people. Socialising or 'networking' in the right places and attending, or even speaking at, the right public events are classic ways for architects to meet their potential clients.

The best way to win work, once established, is to complete high-quality projects and provide an excellent service in the widest sense of the term. A successful project can lead to repeat work for the same client (if they need it), recommendations from clients, recommendations from other collaborators and good relationships all round. A good outcome from a project gives the practice work that can be shown to future prospective clients and enables it to get good references.

Once a practice has a public reputation for successfully delivering a certain type of work then people looking for an architect in that field may approach the company, but a newly established practice cannot expect this. Commonly, architects 'take clients with them', subject to any restrictive employment agreements, when they move from one company to another or leave a firm to set up their own practice.

Planning marketing and business development

Once the practice has identified the market it is targeting, it should develop a marketing and business development plan. This should set out what it is trying to achieve, for example winning certain projects within a given period, then should set a one-, two- or five-year timescale. Any targets should be realistic and achievable within the timescale set. It should set out the marketing material to be produced and the business development activities to be completed.

The purpose of marketing is to get your name, identity and reputation established – called your 'brand' – in the minds of those who matter. A brand is sometimes defined as the visual identity of a company, though it also is the reputation of the product and service behind the name and identity. The new practice should carefully think about its name and visual identity to ensure they convey the intended character of the practice. A comparison with the identities of other successful companies can be a starting point for thinking about how an identity works.

Note that marketing is about listening as well as talking. Information will be needed on potential markets, on specific projects and on what clients and others in the industry think about the practice. Market information can be gleaned from some trade magazines that have sector reports, otherwise the practice will have to glean its own understanding from information gathered online or by talking to people in the sector. The government Department for Business and Trade provides a good service to promote UK companies abroad, including good information about markets and projects. The practice can talk to existing or past clients, or potential clients or consultants, to understand what they want and how they regard the practice.

Keeping in touch

Website

The primary part of a company's public face is its website. The style of the website, the message it conveys by images and words, should be tailored to the market the practice is targeting. People who are searching for an architect may be viewing many websites and may spend only a short time on each one, so the images and words at the front should convey a clear, easily read message. If viewers want to spend more time to find out the detail of the practice's experience, staff, working methods or ideas, that should also be there.

The main elements of the website are normally:

- Introduction to the company – the people, including a summary of their role or experience, not their full CV; the practice philosophy or history.
- Work – the practice's best projects, both past and present. These should be presented with professional photography and the best quality material to illustrate the features the viewer might want to see. Presentation by video is worthwhile for some projects, and professional production should be used to present the projects with impact.
- Contact details – address, phone number and email so that a potential client can easily get in touch. If every staff

member's email address or phone number is on the website they can be pestered by unwanted communications, so the authors would recommend the use of a single central communication phone number and email that can then be picked up in a controlled fashion.

A section giving current news is a good way to keep the website up to the moment, to inform people of the practice's latest achievements and to retain their interest so that they return to the website. This section needs to be kept up to date, probably in line with content on social media.

There are many firms that will design and manage websites for architects and advise on all aspects of structure and presentation. Some architects prefer to design and create their own website for which there are also various potential providers. Some examples are:

Adobe Dreamweaver (www.adobe.com/uk/products/dream weaver)
Squarespace (www.squarespace.com)
Wix (www.wix.com)

These applications offer standard templates and simplified software for typical website features. Some can also host the website, for example Squarespace.

Hosting
Websites are hosted by specialist companies, who offer a variety of levels of services for different requirements.

Getting a domain name

There are various companies that will register a domain name, which can be searched on the internet. They will register the name for use as a website name and for email addresses. Some will offer to host websites and manage email enquiries whilst others offer just registration services. Domain names must be unique, and as for company names, they should not be liable to potential confusion with other companies. The domain name should be thought of as part of the identity of the company as much as the name and visual identity.

Analytics

Google Analytics can report data that website owners may find useful about the number of people visiting a website, which pages they study, how long they 'stay' and their geographical location. Analytics can also link to other Google products to track the progress of advertising campaigns and sales.

Website optimisation

A website can be managed to improve the way it is viewed by search engines, called 'search engine optimisation' (SEO). Thus, certain words that are thought to be the ones people searching might use to find a site can be featured more prominently so that Google and other search engines will pick them up more easily. The people building the website can carry out this optimisation or there are specialist companies who offer the service.

GDPR

The General Data Protection Regulation is a European Union regulation enacted in the UK as the Data Protection Act 2018. The purpose is to protect the individual's personal information and the principle is that a keeper of information cannot store data on an individual unless they have the owner's consent.

The Information Commissioner's Office (ICO) [1] manages a list of keepers of information and processes complaints. If a practice is keeping information on clients, suppliers or contacts, which most practices are, it will need to register with the ICO, for which an annual fee is charged.

Social media

Many companies put information onto social media to ensure their name is in the public eye and to distribute stories about the work and ideas of the practice. Social media can keep a company in the public and professional eye and inform people about current projects or news. Note however a social media presence is not sufficient to win work, and many clients will want to know their architect personally before employing them. Social media can be useful for recruitment, either indirectly by posting that the practice is looking for staff, or directly by approaching potential employees.

LinkedIn

This is the primary social media for business networking. It allows users to find other LinkedIn users and organisations and to be found themselves. They can create a 'profile' including skills, employment, education, recommendations, publications, interests and links to external websites. A user is linked to their 'connections' who can see each other's posts and can message each other. A user's profile can show they are looking for work. Posts can be used to give news and updates.

Instagram and Twitter (X)

These can also be used to give news and updates.

Brochures and similar material, sometimes called 'marketing collateral'

In the past a printed brochure was the core of all practices' marketing material, but this is now being replaced by online material. The author does not see the need for a printed brochure as he expects people may not read it. However, academic publications, books about the practice or company magazines can be valuable in giving a strong support to the company's image.

Some companies like to have other branded goods to give away to keep the company's name in the mind of a potential client, so some companies have pens, bags or other gifts, useful or otherwise, with their name, logo or colours on them to give away.

Thought leadership

Many architects like to think about the type of building in which they specialise: what are the solutions to current problems in the sector? How can the sector respond to the need to reduce carbon emissions? How will the building type develop in the future? Such thoughts can be published if they are worked up into essays, leaflets or books and can be given as lectures or discussions in targeted industry forums.

Working with academia can give time for the development of ideas. Teaching, although probably unlikely to lead to commissions of itself, can be an environment for the development of ideas and contacts.

Conferences

There are conferences or exhibitions for almost all sectors of architecture and design, and in fact every other area of commercial life, so the architect should choose those suited to their company's target market. All of them will charge to attend and many of them will request payment for an opportunity to speak or present or to have a company's name on the conference marketing material as a sponsor. Before attending, the architect should analyse whether the conference will be worth the cost in terms of the benefit it might bring – will they meet people there who will commission work, or will a new contact lead on to an introduction to others who might commission work? Will the architect's presence at the conference promote the company's name amongst those people who matter in the industry? If architects will only be talking to other architects, engineers or consultants similar to themselves this may not be useful, though in some circumstances introductions to clients can come through other consultants.

Advertising

Advertising through the media used by other products and services is not common for architects, however some architects for example place advertisements in magazines that will be read by their target audience. The RIBA Code of Professional Conduct and the ARB The Architects' Code, Standards of Professional Conduct and Practice both set out requirements about the standards to be applied in advertising.

To be effective advertisements should convey a message that can be read in a short time, and they should do this by clear images and words. Professional advertising design will be beneficial.

Photography

Good images of completed buildings are a practice's most valuable resource for future marketing, so it is worthwhile spending time and money on them. The author recommends always using a professional photographer to ensure images are of publishable quality and resolution. Magazines and other publications require high-resolution images with high standards of composition and lighting to maintain the quality of their product. In commissioning photography quality should be prioritised over quantity.

Press coverage

Publication of completed buildings, or articles on individuals in a practice, are a valuable way to promote the company. Articles for publication are best drafted in house and issued as press releases including words and images, as this means the practice can be sure the information contained in them will be correct, and it saves effort for the publication's journalists. More relaxed interfaces with the press such as interviews should be carefully managed to ensure names, data and other information are picked up correctly. If possible, ask to see a copy of the article to check before it is published. Larger practices hire press agencies to handle their relationship with the media.

Costs

All marketing and business development activities will cost money or time, and the overall business plan should account for them. The figure should include all related activities, noting that the largest cost is likely to be people's time. The author is aware of companies allocating around 10% of their turnover each year to be spent on marketing and business development. Whether this figure is right for any particular sector will be a matter of experience – a balance needs to be struck between winning work and doing the work.

Some companies have fallen into the trap of not marketing when they are very busy then running out of work when the busy period ends, whilst others may want to spend more effort on trying to win new work with the aim of trying to grow.

Review of the marketing and business development plan

Like other areas of work the marketing and business development plan should be subject to the process of 'plan, do, review, update'. Questions should be asked honestly of the plan, for example – Were the targets achieved? Which parts of the plan were the most effective and which could be dispensed with? If the targets were not achieved, was the plan wrong or was the target market not really there? Is the plan in fact working, but just taking longer than anticipated? If the plan was partially achieved, would it be worthwhile to change the target to the area where success was found?

Winning a project

The project enquiry

Enquiries to architects from people wanting a designer for a new building come in many forms – from conversations in social settings to advertised requests for proposals for government projects. There are some points to note about all enquiries.

Firstly the practice principals should ask: 'Does the practice want to take on the project?' This question can be broken down into sub-questions:

Will the practice make money from the project? By identifying the work involved and the potential fees the profitability can be estimated.

How much will it cost the practice to make the proposal, particularly if it includes a design submission? Does the practice have the time and money to make the bid?

Does the practice have the ability to carry out the work? If it does not have the ability now, can it acquire the people, equipment and process within the required time to do so?

Does the project fit in with the practice's profile for its work? Note that the types of projects that the practice has planned to carry out might not be what clients want it to do, so the practice might move towards different areas of work as it finds out what the market wants.

Does the practice want to work for this client?

Is the practice likely to win the bidding process?

The practice should review the chance of winning the project before deciding to bid. Public, open submissions are likely to have the largest number of bidders, so each practice is less likely to win them compared to invited submissions. The fewer the number of invited practices the better the chance of winning, and the best requests for proposal are the ones for which there is only one bidder.

Some submissions will be called 'competitions' where there might be a design element in the submission. The author's experience is that in open public design competitions there are too many participants for there to be an acceptable like-lihood of winning. Invited design competitions with three to six invitees would be judged a better risk for the participants.

The practice should find out about the project and the client in order to make the decision about whether to proceed with a submission for the potential project. It can look at similar pro-jects that have been completed in the locality or in comparable locations to find out how long they took, how much they cost, what the problems were. If anyone in the practice knows other consultants, contractors or other contacts who were involved in similar buildings they can be useful to give insight into what went well and what did not.

The architect should ask whether the information given in the request for proposal is clear:

Is the project scope fully identified?

Is the project schedule fully identified?

What will be the contractor procurement method?

Is the site clearly shown and does the client own it?

What are the terms of the appointment?

The practice should educate itself about potential clients. As well as finding out about them as individuals, it is important to find out about their financial position whether they are private individuals, companies or government organisations. How are they going to pay for the project, and do they really have the money? Can any insight be gained into what they want of the project? What sort of client will they be – will they be a decisive decision-maker or will all decisions have to go through long review by a committee? How a client makes decisions can have a strong influence on how quickly the design work proceeds.

The architect should know important information about the potential client and the project by the time he or she makes the submission:

> What does the client want from the project? What will be the likely cost of the building? When does the client want the building designed and completed? What quality of building is required?

The architect should aim to know about the client and to understand their potential project better than they do.

The written submission

The written submission should be tailored to suit the client. In their research described in the previous paragraphs the architect will have found out about the client's priorities and interests. The proposal should respond to these and answer the questions they will want to know about.

Requests for proposals come in many forms:

Capability submission.
Capability and fee submission.
Capability, working method and fee submission,
Design submission along with capability, method and fee.

Each of these might be an open request for proposal or might be invited. They might be in one, two or more stages – capability submission, then a fee submission for a selected shortlist, or capability and fee submission then an interview for a selected shortlist – and the submission might be by written proposal only or include an interview. The design submission, otherwise known as a design competition, might be paid or not.

In order to make the proposal the architect will have to:

Identify the project scope and deliverables as described in Chapter 9 Project delivery;

Prepare a project programme as described in Chapter 9 Project delivery;

Prepare a staffing plan for the project as described in Chapter 6 People management;

Calculate a fee for the project as described in Chapter 7 Finances;

Identify any other consultants required and obtain their costs based on their identified scope and staffing. To do this a design responsibility matrix can be prepared as described in Chapter 9 Project delivery;

Prepare an overall project fee proposal as described in Chapter 7 Finances;

Prepare a report or memorandum setting out all of the aforementioned, either for inclusion in the submission or for internal records if the submission requests only the main conclusions.

The written proposal should focus on answering the client's needs rather than talking about the bidding architect. The following is the contents of a typical written submission:

Introduction thanking the client for requesting the proposal from the practice;

Understanding of the project, repeating back what the architect has understood is the scope of the project. This might fill in the gaps in the information provided in the request for proposal;

Design submission, if any;

Working method setting out the programme, staffing, project processes and so forth as asked for in the request for proposal;

Fee proposal;

Practice profile and staff CVs.

The written document should make the maximum use of images of the practice's best similar past projects.

Interviews

An interview is the opportunity for the architect to make contact with the client in person. They will, for most projects, have to work with their architect for a period of years, so they will want to know the architect can do the work and they are trustworthy and maybe even likeable. The client will gain an impression the moment the architect walks into the room, and maybe before then with the communications in the run-up to the interview. Communications should be efficient and pleasant without being effusive or false.

The architect should find out about their client, what they want and how they work, so the presentation can be tailored to the potential employer's character. As with the written proposal, a presentation in an interview should emphasise solving the client's problems, not talking about the architect themselves.

Small matters can be important, so the architect should arrive promptly, take no longer than the time allocated, talk clearly and present the matters they have been asked to do.

Reference

[1] The Information Commissioner's Office. https://ico.org.uk

6
People management

Introduction

Every practice should aim to create a happy, motivated team with the right mix of people doing the tasks appropriate to their skills and experience. The senior principals in the practice will need to plan out the hiring and management of the people in the office on their projects and offer leadership. This chapter discusses the subjects of allocating existing employees as well as hiring new staff and then managing the team throughout the duration of a project.

When a practice is appointed to a project it must ensure it can make available an adequate number of people who between them hold the necessary skills to carry out the work. Once the individuals are allocated to the work, they must be managed to complete the work to the appropriate standard. The RIBA Code of Professional Conduct includes several clauses regarding relationships with employees.

The law surrounding employment is extensive, and if a practice would like assistance with HR matters:

- The RIBA offers HR and employment law services under its RIBA Business heading;
- The employment section of the government website contains useful links on employment matters [1];
- The Labour Relations Agency provides information on employment matters [2];
- There are specialist HR consultancy firms that can offer advice;

DOI: 10.4324/9781003327288-8

- In Chapter 14 Computing we mention an example of an HR software package that includes consultancy advice as part of the subscription.

Hiring

There are various ways for a practice to find people who might be suitable for employment:

- Unsolicited enquiries may from time to time be received from applicants wanting to work at the practice, some of whom may have investigated the practice and found they would like to work there. If so, they could be suitable for and compatible with the company.
- Recommendations from colleagues, both within the office and across the profession and industry, can provide an invaluable source of suitable candidates for consideration.
- Advertising. Advertisements can be placed in the trade journals and on social media or websites, including the RIBA's website; as well as attracting applicants for consideration, these can often be regarded as useful in raising the profile of the practice more generally. Online advertisements can be placed through websites, for example magazine websites, social media and the practice's own website.
- Agencies. There are various recruitment and employment agencies, including RIBA Jobs [3], that will assemble shortlists of candidates who can be interviewed for employment by the practice or, in some cases, supply staff who will be employed by the agency and work for the practice. People employed by an agency will tend to be on a short-term basis where they are paid by the hours worked.
- Recruitment agencies will find candidates to match the requirements identified by the practice, and they may have a list of people on their books, so saving time and effort. They will charge for their service; when they are finding individuals for employment their fee is normally at a percentage

of the annual starting salary of candidates employed, when they are placing their own staff in a practice their fee will be a percentage of the employee's hourly rate.

- Headhunting. Sometimes people who are already in employment can be approached to fill a particular staffing requirement, a process that is normally used for more senior or specialist staff. Some agencies can also offer a headhunting service.
- Personal contacts. Good people can be found through contacts in the personal networks of the practice principals or staff.
- Employees can be hired directly from university so visiting student end-of-year shows, teaching, examining, or attending project 'crits' can be seen as ways to spot future talent.

Diversity and inclusion

Take care to ensure searching for potential employees from your own network or elsewhere does not restrict diversity and inclusion in the workplace. The recruitment processes can be structured to reduce any potential bias in terms of inclusion and some methods are likely to bring in a broader diversity of people – unsolicited enquiries or meeting university students for example. CVs can then be reviewed 'blind', that is without knowing the name of the applicant or anything about them. Bias can also occur when interviewing, though it can be avoided if you are aware of it. Apart from any wider social dis-benefit, bias in recruitment would reduce the range of talent available to the practice and would be contrary to the RIBA chartered practice Equality, Diversity and Inclusion policy.

The employment specification

To find the right person a specification should be written identifying:

- The required skills including different design skills, project management, BIM;
- The level of experience required in designing and managing specific types of projects;
- The qualifications required;
- The basis of employment; the location, temporary or permanent, the level of salary, other benefits;
- Any other personal qualities.

Interviewing

Once the applicants have been sifted to find a shortlist of those that most closely fit the requirements an interview process should be followed. Note that employing people who have the wrong skills, experience or attitude or who are incompatible in some way can be expensive and take some effort to undo, so it is important that the interview process should be thorough and reliable. Some recommendations for this process are:

- Set a list of criteria against which the candidate will be judged and key questions to be asked;
- Candidates should be interviewed by more than one person wherever possible, and it is best if they are seen by the senior manager who will be working with them;
- A structured approach to interviews with appropriate questions rather than an off-the-cuff conversation;
- If candidates are being interviewed by more than one person, those people should confer together to ensure a consistency of approach;
- Consider setting tests to gauge candidates' competence in BIM or other skills.

The purpose of an interview is for the company to find out more about the candidate, and also, importantly, for the candidate to find out more about the company, its culture, and its people. Through conversation the candidate's knowledge and ability to communicate can be compared with their curriculum vitae, and the interviewers can get a better understanding of how much the candidate will fit in within the office. For employment to be a successful relationship the candidate must want to work in the practice and the members of the office must be happy working with any new recruit.

The basis of employment

Staff can be employed on a full-time basis, on a temporary basis (for a number of days, weeks or months to perform a particular task) or on a part-time basis (for less than the full number of hours a week). Other methods of employment include agency staff (where the person is employed by the agency who is then responsible for their terms of employment) and self-employed staff or consultants. Note that if self-employed people work almost exclusively, or exclusively, for one practice, the tax authorities may deem them to be employees and challenge the status of their employment and associated taxation arrangements.

The employment contract

The employment contract should be available in draft during the interview process and concluded before the employee starts work, but certainly no later than one month after commencement of work.

The employment contract should include:

- Details of the employer and employee;
- Dates of commencement of work, including any probationary period, and the date of the end of employment, which will be the date of retirement in a permanent contract;
- The role including any specific duties;
- The place of work, including any requirements for work away from that location;

- Hours of work;
- Details of payment including overtime payment arrangements, if any;
- Pension arrangements;
- Sickness benefits, maternity and paternity leave, time off for CPD, training or other reasons;
- Any other benefits such as health insurance, annual subscriptions to the profession's institute and registration board, food provided by the office, loans for season tickets, parking and the like;
- Termination: the notice period (from the employer and employee) and processes related to termination including pay in lieu of notice or 'gardening leave' (paid absence from the office during the notice period);
- Disciplinary procedures and grievance procedures.

The contract might also include:

- Requirements for confidentiality to protect the practice's work and their contracts with clients which might in turn contain confidentiality clauses;
- Intellectual property: the employee should acknowledge that the work he or she produces is the property of the company;
- Restrictive covenants for the period after the employee has left the company, which are more commonly used for senior employees. These will apply for a fixed period after leaving and might include a requirement not to approach existing clients or to poach staff. Legal advice should be taken regarding the operation and drafting of these clauses;
- Training: a commitment to staff training and CPD.

Note that employment contracts are fairly standard documents, and legally compliant templates can be obtained from legal firms.

Once employed the employee has the right to receive a written statement of the employment particulars, separate from their contract, setting out all the conditions of employment and covering pensions, collective agreements, training, and disciplinary and grievance procedures.

Employees have rights to protect them against discrimination on the grounds of sexual orientation, race, age, disability, religion, pregnancy or working arrangements. Employees have also many rights in law in relation to whistleblowing, dismissal, redundancy, holidays, maternity and paternity leave and provisions, trade union representation and other matters. Further information on these matters can be found in the sources referred to in the introduction to this chapter.

Where appropriate more in-depth advice on the extensive topic of employment law should be sought from experienced lawyers or specialists.

Employing non-UK nationals

Non-UK nationals will generally require a right to work in some form to be employed in the UK. In order to employ someone from outside the UK the practice will require a sponsor licence. Information about sponsor licences can be found on the UK government website [4]. This also lists the categories of people who do not need sponsorship.

Retirement

Employers used to be able to enforce retirement at 65, but this right was withdrawn in 2011 and now employees have the right to work to whatever age they would like or are capable.

Health and safety at work

The Health and Safety at Work Act 1974 places a duty on the employer to do all that is reasonably practical to ensure the health, safety and welfare of employees and others whilst in the company's premises and away from the premises or on site whilst on company business. It also places a duty on employees to take reasonable care for their own safety.

Insurance

When a company employs staff it is legally required to take out employer's liability insurance to provide compensation to staff who may be injured in the course of their work or suffer a work-related illness. The insurance must have a minimum cover of £5 million.

Pensions

Under the Pensions Act 2008, when a company employs staff over the age of 22 up to state pension age and earning more than £10,000 per year, it is required to enrol them in a pension scheme. The employer can delay the start of the scheme no longer than three months after the employee's commencement. The employer and employee together have to pay at least 8% of the staff member's salary into the pension scheme, of which the employer has to contribute at least 3% of the employee's salary.

Staff handbook

It can be helpful to set out the conditions of employment and related matters in a staff handbook. Much of the information in this will not be contractual so can be updated when needed, and indeed a staff handbook should be regarded as a live document to be kept current. As well as including standard employment conditions and benefits including health insurance, bonuses, office CPD and similar matters discussed earlier, the handbook could contain procedures for submitting timesheets, for claiming expenses, for making complaints;

health and safety information and procedures for visiting sites; and other practice policies that staff should be aware of. The staff handbook should be kept easily available.

Managing people

For a company to work effectively and happily, management and leadership are required.

'People management' consists of setting a framework for people to work within to ensure they produce the results required within the timescale available. Leadership consists of setting the goals for people to achieve, inspiring them with ideas, setting an example to be followed by the company and supporting people when they need it.

In the author's experience when staff are asked what would help them in their work they say they want to be told what is expected of them. Primarily this means people want to understand clearly what work they are being asked to do and when they should complete it. To be able to give clear instructions the senior person leading the project should plan out the work: firstly, what are the tasks that need to be done? Secondly, what is the timescale in which they should be completed?

The plan of work should identify the major tasks to be done on a project and split them into sections that can be done by one person. On a large project one person may be allocated solely to that job and be given a seemingly small part – designing cores, scheduling doors or similar – whereas if projects are small enough one person may be able to handle the whole project, or even all aspects of several whole projects at once.

The tasks should be distributed to the people who are most suited to them – people with more experience should handle the more complex tasks; people who are good communicators and have good judgement can handle the meetings and relationships; those with a technical experience in one area should work in that field; and staff who are more junior should work in a role where they are overseen by senior members of the team.

Some people work more quickly than others or manage their own work in different ways, so the project manager needs to understand how the different people in the office work to construct a team that will work together productively. Table 6.1 shows a typical staffing plan allocating people to tasks for 6 weeks of a project.

In parallel with splitting up the tasks between the team, the manager should produce a programme setting out the timescale for each task and the order in which those tasks are to be carried out. Some people may think they instinctively know what to do and when to do it, however planning out the tasks and timescale carefully in a clear graphic will help ensure that there is no misunderstanding about objectives and the timing of delivery for the various work 'parcels'. In the author's experience time spent planning out work is never wasted.

The staffing plan needs to be developed in parallel with the project fees described in Chapter 7 Finances. The resource allocation and time planning should match the available fees. Once established the staffing plan should then be monitored against the fee schedule as the project progresses to ensure the people and money remain aligned.

Programmes are discussed further in Chapter 9 Project delivery. In Chapter 14 Computing we identify software packages to assist in project programming. These allow people to be allocated to tasks in the programme.

People management is about communication and once the tasks and timescales are planned out they must be clearly communicated to the team. Everyone on the programme should have the opportunity to comment on the work and timescales, so that they understand their work and have a sense of 'ownership' of the programme.

Table 3.1 A typical staffing plan for RIBA Stages 1 and 2 of a project

| | Stage 1 Preparation and Briefing | | | | | | Stage 2 Concept Design | | | | | | | | | | | | Total hours per task |
| | Week 1 | | | Week 2 | | | Week 3 | | | Week 4 | | | Week 5 | | | Week 6 | | | |
Person / Task	Xavier	Yasmine	Zachary	Xavier	Yasmine	Zachary	Xavier	Yasmine	Zachary	Xavier	Yasmine	Zachary	Xavier	Yasmine	Zachary	Xavier	Yasmine	Zachary	
Meetings																			
Project planning	7			7															14
Client meeting	3			3			3			3			3			3			18
Client presentation							4	4		4	4		4	4		4	4		32
Team meeting	3	3	3	3	3	3	3	3	3	3	3	3	3	3	3	3	3	3	54
Project set-up																			
Project set-up admin		4																	4
Project set-up CAD			7																7
Briefing and site investigation																			
Investigation of planning		10			14														24
Site survey		7	7		7	7													28
Brief writing	7	7	23	7	7	30													81
Design																			
Concept design workshop							7	7	7										21
Concept design drawings							3	17	30	10	24	37	10	24	37				192
Preparation of concept deign report																30	24	37	91
Total hours	20	31	40	20	31	40	20	31	40	20	31	40	20	31	40	40	31	40	566
Percentage of time	50%	78%	100%	50%	78%	100%	50%	78%	100%	50%	78%	100%	50%	78%	100%	100%	78%	100%	100%

Once produced, plans must be monitored and updated in a cycle described as 'plan, do, review, adjust'. See Chapter 9 Project delivery on the monitoring of the programme.

Leadership

This is a more intangible quality, and one that is not discussed as often as management is. It consists in giving direction to both a project and a company and in setting an example through work and behaviour. The personal characters of the leaders of a company and their behaviour will set the tone of the whole organisation.

It should be noted that the RIBA Code of Practice and the ARB's Architects Code, Standards of Professional Conduct and Practice both talk about standards of behaviour including fairness, honesty, confidentiality and integrity, additional to the actions and administration required for architectural practice.

The leaders of a practice should set out the aims of the organisation in terms of philosophy, design, future targets, office space, staff and other matters that affect the employees. These should be clearly communicated to everyone in so far as they affect them, and each person should understand their part in the whole. The directors may, of course, not wish to communicate the finances of the company, sensitive information about future projects and similar items to everyone, though the author would recommend staff understand the finances of the project they are allocated to.

Having a company that is working efficiently is partly about having a team that is motivated, capable, satisfied and happy.

Staff are likely to be more motivated if they are working on interesting projects that are well designed. They should understand the design philosophy they are applying. Additional to the design of the projects, well-managed projects in a well-managed office have a strong management structure that will enable people to carry out their own work efficiently.

Again, most people will be happy if they feel they are valued by the company, not only in terms of pay, benefits and conditions, but also in terms of the way they are treated. If communications from the senior staff are clear, timely and respectful team members should respond well; if however, those communications are ambiguous or contradictory, late or patronising they may feel aggrieved, complain either in private or openly and feel discouraged. Encouragement and recognition of hard work or important contributions is always appreciated.

Staff should be supported both in their day-to-day work and in their longer-term development. When staff members have a problem that affects their work and performance, they will be reassured to know that senior people are available to assist them. Critical or erratic responses to requests for assistance can be very de-motivating and should be avoided.

Staff should be offered the training, support and resources that they need to progress their work (for example, appropriate software and when necessary instruction and tuition in its use). Support should also be constantly available in terms of meeting the CPD requirements of the RIBA and ARB. All staff should be offered training to develop their careers. This will also benefit the overall skills base of the office, including management training for those likely to be moving onto a management role in the company.

Most employees will also appreciate the provision of a personalised career structure within the company. If they feel reassured that by working and contributing well towards the success of the company they will be rewarded with promotion, most staff members will be incentivised to optimise their effort and performance.

Many companies have regular, normally annual, staff reviews. These are fairly formal meetings between staff and management that give both parties an opportunity to talk about their relationship. The team leaders can talk about how the team member is getting on and what they see for them in the future.

The team member can discuss the good and bad of their work and what they would like to do in the future. Companies find this process useful as issues can be discussed in this forum that might not be brought up at any other time. The review can be recorded and become part of the career development structure in the office if desired.

Some companies choose to distribute profits or shares in the company to members of staff, either as part of promotion to more senior positions within the company or simply as part of the basic terms of employment. Share-related schemes offer to those invited to participate a stake in the success of the organisation.

Company-wide meetings, sector and team meetings, and where appropriate discrete office meetings, as well as social events, can contribute significantly to creating a positive and successful working environment within a company. Company-wide meetings, which will be possible in all but the largest companies, sector, team and office meetings should help to ensure the whole organisation is kept up to date with current projects and the overall progress and direction of the company. Information can be distributed through the company also by intranets, company websites pages and messages to staff. Social events can be very effective in helping people to relax and get to know each other and in building 'team spirit' within the office.

Difficult situations

Things can go wrong in the office so, although the ways in which problems can arise are inevitably highly varied, an open discussion about a problem will often assist with resolution if it is handled with fairness, sensitivity and appropriate levels of confidentiality where required. Specialist employment advice should be sought where the problems go beyond those matters of relationship or other simpler issues that can be dealt with easily by the senior people in the office. This advice can be from experienced HR managers or consultants, specialist organisations or, if needed, lawyers.

References

[1] The Employment Section of the UK Government. https://www.gov.uk/browse/working
[2] The Labour Relations Agency. https://www.lra.org.uk
[3] Job Advertisement Through the RIBA. https://jobs.architecture.com
[4] Information About International Employment Sponsor Licences. https://www.gov.uk/uk-visa-sponsorship-employers

7
Finances

Introduction

This chapter sets out the main principles of financial management of a business, firstly of the office as a whole, then of the projects, noting that the finances of the office are to a large extent consequent on the performance of the individual projects in progress at any one time.

The chapter sets out the financial information the architect will need to know as a foundation for a business, however all practices are recommended to also employ an accountant to manage their taxes and annual accounts as a minimum and to give them advice on management and optimisation of their business.

The starting point of financial management is to have a plan for the year ahead. This allows decisions to be made about spending based on knowledge of the projected income. A plan can also be produced for two- or five-year intervals, although the further ahead the figures are projected the less reliable they are likely to be. Table 7.1 shows a typical annual financial plan spreadsheet.

Architects in practice offer a professional service the successful provision of which is reliant upon the application of their skills and knowledge, which they provide in return for a fee. There are various ways in which that fee might be calculated that are discussed later: as a percentage of the construction cost of the building; as a time charge; as a fixed lump sum; or as a share of the profit on the project. The key to control of practice finances is the control of time spent on projects and of time spent on non-fee-earning activities.

DOI: 10.4324/9781003327288-9

This chapter will also give an outline of the different taxes payable in a typical limited company structure.

The practice finances

The basic point of managing the finances of a company is to ensure that outgoings are equal to or less than income. It is to be noted that many businesses that fail economically are notionally profitable; they are just caught out by running out of cash. This is a problem of timing – there is money being earned on projects or even invoiced, but since the cash has not been received and money has been paid out, the bank account has run out of money. Insolvency results from the inability to pay debts or meet financial obligations as and when they arise. Therefore, income and outgoings need to balance in the long term in the annual financial plan, and they also need to work in the short term by leaving the bank balance positive at all times. The author is aware of companies that manage their annual finances against a managed overdraft that is repaid at the end of each financial year. However he would advise against this arrangement due partly to its additional cost, and more importantly as the company must be certain of its income to ensure it will be able to pay off the debt each 12 months, something not easy for most practices. The accountants saying – 'Turnover is vanity, profit is sanity, and cash is king' – should be remembered!

Income

Income usually arrives purely from projects, although some staff members may bring in other income to the business from other activities such as teaching or writing. Some architects also act as developers or waive early fees in return for a share in development profits.

Outgoings

These should firstly be classified as either 'project costs' or
'overheads':

Project costs are those required to complete the work on each
particular project. They typically comprise:

- Staff time spent on the project;
- Travel;
- Computing and printing costs;
- Sub-consultant costs.

Overheads are then all other costs to make the practice function, typically:

- Architects' time spent on non-project work such as office
  management and business development;
- Employees who do not work directly on fee-earning pro-
  jects, such as secretaries, in-house accountants, office
  managers;
- External support such as auditors and accountants;
- Office costs such as rent, utilities, furniture, coffee;
- IT;
- Insurances.

Overheads can be classified as fixed and variable. Fixed costs
are those that cannot be varied month to month; variable
costs are those that can be adjusted. Fixed overheads are
typically:

- Overhead staff time;
- Office rent;
- Insurance;
- Other rental agreements such as IT and furniture;
- Accountants' fees.

Variable overheads are typically:

- Staff time spent on non-project work;
- Training;
- Utilities;
- Other incidental costs.

Overhead and profit rates

Overheads are normally identified as a proportion of the project costs, for example if the project costs are £1,000 per month and the overheads are £500, then the overheads are described as 50%, or 0.5 of project costs. The rate of overheads varies enormously between companies with some as low as around 0.25 times costs, and the author has heard of companies whose overheads were as much as five times costs. A general rule of thumb indicating a normal balance of these figures is project costs = overhead = profit. This means the total fee is three times the base costs, however each company should analyse their overheads to ensure they have the right balance of profitability with a price level that is acceptable to their clients. Obviously, lower overheads mean the practice has more to spend on carrying out the work and more money as profit after all project and overhead costs have been accounted for.

Profit

HMRC defines profit as the money remaining after all legitimate project and overhead costs are paid, and they will apply corporation tax to this figure. Unfortunately, even after tax, this money is not all available to the owners of the practice as their annual bonus. The most important function of 'profit' is to act as a cash reserve to allow the next projects to be won and to allow the work on them to be financed until cash is received, noting what has been explained earlier about the timing of payment.

Profit can also be utilised to pay for any investments, for example in new equipment, offices and expansion of the company. Such investments may attract tax relief. The author would advise the reader to be cautious about taking too much money out of the company for bonuses. Notwithstanding any organised loan or overdraft facilities, it is generally good policy for the managers to retain a reserve in the company's bank account sufficient to pay all the company's costs for, perhaps, three months if the practice is confident about a continuing stream of work coming into the company, or nine months to a year if it is more unsure about when the next project will arrive. This reserve will also enable the company to continue to pay staff and overheads without receiving any income for a period, or pay for staff redundancies if the next project does not appear.

Tax

An architectural practice will be obliged to pay a variety of taxes against its business operation. These are listed next.

The rates of tax and methods of calculation of each category of taxation are occasionally varied by HMRC as part of the economic policies introduced by government, so they should be checked every time the company fills in the relevant tax submission, and for all but the simplest company accounts the management of these various tax returns and submissions is best placed in the hands of a qualified accountant.

On fees charged

Value-added tax, when the business is VAT registered, is chargeable on fees and is calculated as 20% on top of the total fees. VAT on sales (Output VAT) is therefore collected by the business, and paid to HMRC (usually) on a quarterly basis, but with the benefit of being able to offset from this VAT paid on allowable business expenses (Input VAT) via the preparation and submission of a VAT return.

Table 7.1 A typical annual financial plan

			April	May	June	July	August
Income							
Projects							
101 Auspicious Ltd.				25,000.00	25,000.00	25,000.00	25,000.0
102 Beautiful House				35,000.00	35,000.00	10,000.00	10,000.0
103 Copious refurbishment				12,500.00	12,500.00	12,500.00	12,500.0
104 D (Potential)					25,000.00	50,000.00	50,000.0
105 E (Potential)							12,500.0
TOTAL Receipts				72,500.00	97,500.00	97,500.00	1,10,000.0
Outgoings							
Staff	Salary	Adjusted salary					
Valery	60,000.00	73,800.00	6,150.00	6,150.00	6,150.00	6,150.00	6,150.0
William	50,000.00	61,500.00	5,125.00	5,125.00	5,125.00	5,125.00	5,125.C
Xavier	50,000.00	61,500.00	5,125.00	5,125.00	5,125.00	5,125.00	5,125.C
Yasmine	35,000.00	43,050.00	3,587.50	3,587.50	3,587.50	3,587.50	3,587.5
Zachary	25,000.00	30,750.00	2,562.50	2,562.50	2,562.50	2,562.50	2,562.5
TOTAL salaries			22,550.00	22,550.00	22,550.00	22,550.00	22,550.C
Pay rise	3%						
TOTAL pay			22,550.00	22,550.00	22,550.00	22,550.00	22,550.C
Sub-consultants							
Usman							12,000.0
Landscape			6,000.00	6,000.00	6,000.00	12,000.00	
TOTAL Sub-consultants			6,000.00	6,000.00	6,000.00	12,000.00	12,000.C
Overheads							
Other project-specific costs			2,500.00	2,500.00	2,500.00	2,500.00	2,500.C
Office rent			12,500.00	12,500.00	12,500.00	12,500.00	12,500.C
Utilities			3,147.00	3,147.00	3,147.00	3,147.00	3,147.C
Office running costs			500.00	500.00	500.00	500.00	500.C
Computers and software			500.00	500.00	500.00	500.00	500.0
Accountant			600.00	600.00	600.00	600.00	600.C
Insurance			22,000.00				
Marketing			4,000.00	4,000.00	4,000.00	4,000.00	4,000.C
Contingency			1,500.00	1,500.00	1,500.00	1,500.00	1,500.0
TOTAL costs			47,247.00	25,247.00	25,247.00	25,247.00	25,247.C
Profit and loss							
Income			72,500.00	97,500.00	97,500.00	97,500.00	1,10,000.C
Profit (Income less salaries, sub-consultants and overheads)			−3,297.00	43,703.00	43,703.00	37,703.00	50,203.C
Corporation tax	25%			0.00	10,925.75	10,925.75	9,425.75	12,550.7
Nett profit			−3,297.00	32,777.25	32,777.25	28,277.25	37,652.2

Note: This plan does not account for VAT which will be added to the invoices in circumstances where VAT is applicable.

September	October	November	December	January	February	March	Totals
25,000.00	25,000.00	25,000.00	25,000.00	25,000.00	0.00	0.00	2,50,000.00
35,000.00	35,000.00	35,000.00	35,000.00	35,000.00	35,000.00	35,000.00	3,45,000.00
25,000.00	25,000.00	25,000.00	25,000.00	25,000.00	25,000.00	25,000.00	2,37,500.00
12,500.00							1,87,500.00
12,500.00	12,500.00	12,500.00	12,500.00	12,500.00	12,500.00	12,500.00	1,00,000.00
1,10,000.00	97,500.00	97,500.00	97,500.00	97,500.00	72,500.00	72,500.00	11,20,000.00
6,150.00	6,150.00	6,150.00	6,150.00	6,150.00	6,150.00	6,150.00	
5,125.00	5,125.00	5,125.00	5,125.00	5,125.00	5,125.00	5,125.00	
5,125.00	5,125.00	5,125.00	5,125.00	5,125.00	5,125.00	5,125.00	
3,587.50	3,587.50	3,587.50	3,587.50	3,587.50	3,587.50	3,587.50	
2,562.50	2,562.50	2,562.50	2,562.50	2,562.50	2,562.50	2,562.50	
22,550.00	22,550.00	22,550.00	22,550.00	22,550.00	22,550.00	22,550.00	2,70,600.00
				676.50	676.50	676.50	
22,550.00	22,550.00	22,550.00	22,550.00	23,226.50	23,226.50	23,226.50	2,72,629.50
12,000.00	12,000.00						
		6,000.00	6,000.00	6,000.00			
12,000.00	12,000.00	6,000.00	6,000.00	6,000.00	0.00	0.00	84,000.00
2,500.00	2,500.00	2,500.00	2,500.00	2,500.00	2,500.00	2,500.00	30,000.00
12,500.00	12,500.00	12,500.00	12,500.00	15,000.00	15,000.00	15,000.00	1,57,500.00
3,147.00	3,147.00	3,147.00	3,147.00	3,147.00	3,147.00	3,147.00	
500.00	500.00	500.00	500.00	500.00	500.00	500.00	
500.00	500.00	500.00	500.00	500.00	500.00	500.00	6,000.00
600.00	600.00	600.00	600.00	600.00	600.00	600.00	7,200.00
							22,000.00
4,000.00	4,000.00	4,000.00	4,000.00	4,000.00	4,000.00	4,000.00	48,000.00
1,500.00	1,500.00	1,500.00	1,500.00	1,500.00	1,500.00	1,500.00	18,000.00
25,247.00	25,247.00	25,247.00	25,247.00	27,747.00	27,747.00	27,747.00	3,32,464.00
1,10,000.00	97,500.00	97,500.00	97,500.00	97,500.00	72,500.00	72,500.00	11,20,000.00
50,203.00	37,703.00	43,703.00	43,703.00	40,526.50	21,526.50	21,526.50	4,30,906.50
12,550.75	9,425.75	10,925.75	10,925.75	10,131.63	5,381.63	5,381.63	1,08,550.88
37,652.25	28,277.25	32,777.25	32,777.25	30,394.88	16,144.88	16,144.88	3,22,355.63

Businesses are liable to charge VAT on their fees if their VAT taxable turnover is greater than £90,000 (figure correct as of 1 April 2024). At the point the business has an expectation that it will exceed this income level on a future basis, it must register with HMRC for VAT purposes to obtain a VAT Registration Number that will enable it to make the required VAT returns.

When proposing a fee it is important to identify to the client whether the figure includes VAT. Fees are often quoted without VAT, and if this is done a note such as 'ex VAT' should be clearly written by the fee figure to indicate that it does not include tax. The VAT should then be added to every invoice issued.

Work on projects outside the United Kingdom does not generally attract UK VAT. This rule applies if the building to be designed is outside the UK; it is not dependent on the location of the office carrying out the work or on the location of the client. However, if the work abroad comprises consultancy services that are not related to a specific site and the client is UK-based, the work may then attract VAT. Fees on work abroad may also attract local VAT or equivalent, withholding tax, or other local taxes and these should in each case be checked with a taxation specialist with experience appropriate to the location. VAT is a particularly complex area and notwithstanding the aforementioned, the author's advice is to always seek professional advice from your qualified accountant.

On salaries

Income tax is payable by employees on their salaries, and national insurance (NI) is payable by both the employee and employer on such salaries. These taxes, both the employees' and employer's contributions, are deducted and covered by the employer and paid through HMRC's 'pay as you earn' (PAYE) scheme which is managed either by the employer or by a specialist company engaged to perform this 'payroll' service. Such PAYE returns usually require monthly submission.

Note that the rates of income tax to be paid on different rates of salaries are complicated and are subject to regular change so are best left for a qualified accountant or payroll provider to calculate and check. Most firms of accountants will offer payroll services.

On profits
Corporation tax is payable by all companies on the tax-adjusted profit of the company, after making due allowance for capital investment (e.g. IT equipment).

On dividends
Dividends paid to shareholders of a company attract income tax charged at a rate dependent on the income tax rate relevant to the proportion of tax payable as 'basic rate', or 'higher rate' income for the individual, submitted to HMRC via the recipient's personal tax return.

On other activities
If the business disposes of 'investment' assets such as property, the disposal will attract capital gains tax (CGT), which is broadly payable on the difference between the initial purchase price and the subsequent disposal price of the asset. For a company the CGT rate is equivalent to the corporation tax rate. For LLPs, sole traders and partnerships the rates differ, so advice should be taken from a qualified accountant.

Accounts

Private limited companies are required to submit annual financial statements to Companies House and an annual corporation tax return to HMRC. The accounts to Companies House must normally be filed within nine months of the end of a company's financial year. The deadline for the corporation tax return is 12 months after the end of the company's financial year, albeit strangely the corporation tax payment is normally due by nine months and one day after the year end.

Sole traders and partnerships are also obliged to prepare accounts in order to complete their required tax returns, although such accounts do not need to be filed in the public domain. Note, LLPs are required to file their accounts in the public domain at Companies House.

Small business accounts (sole trader and partnership) can be presented on the basis of two different ways of recognising income, known as 'cash' and 'accruals':

Cash: income and expenses are recognised in the accounts when the cash is received or paid.
Accruals: income and expenses are recognised when the in-voice is issued to the client or received from the supplier, irrespective of when the payment is ultimately made or received.
Note that accounts of larger companies must be presented in the 'accruals' format. The rules on using either basis, or the pros and cons of each, should be discussed with your external accountant.

It is important to keep a close review of a practice's ongoing financial position in order to ensure that costs do not get off track and therefore to keep the correct relationship between income and costs. A financial report should be prepared at the end of each month, or more frequently if needed, setting out income and outgoings for the period. A key component of the 'management accounts' will be the cashflow forecast, a key calculation to help the business owners run and manage the business's finances going forward.

The financial plan for the year ahead (see Table 7.1) sets out the expected trajectory of income, project costs and over-heads. These will all change as the year progresses, so the annual financial plan should be updated every three months with actual performance reviewed against the plan to enable the business owner to understand how the business is performing.

Reporting

The practice should establish a regular pattern of reports so that those managing it can see what is happening financially in the company, and most importantly, so that they can identify potential problems as early as possible. These should have a headlines section that can be easily digested and backup information for those who want to read the detail.

Monthly reports

These should show:

- Headline overall profitability;
- The cash balance – money in and out;
- Unpaid invoices, and those issued;
- Project reports for each project showing progress and profitability;
- Comparison against the annual forecast for the company;
- Comparison against the forecasts for each project.

The report might also show other measures, sometimes called 'key performance indicators' (KPIs) such as:

- Income or profit by partner, fee earner or others;
- Income or profit by group or sector, project type, client or others;
- Creditor and debtor days – how long it takes to pay or be paid.

Annual reports

The contents of these must follow statutory requirements if they are to be submitted to Companies House. Additionally the practice should produce a report for those managing it, including:

- A summary section covering the metrics they find most useful;
- The full report compiling together the monthly reports;
- A comparison of the performance against the annual forecast; and
- An updated forecast for the next period.

Project finances

The income of the practice is the sum of the net fees for all the projects plus any income from other sources. The fees for any individual project therefore need to pay for the work to be done on the project, plus when added together the fees for all the projects in the office need to include enough income to cover all the overheads and the support and administrative work done in the office that is not fee earning, and above that still return some profit for the business.

Calculating the fees for a project

The fees are normally established at the beginning of a project by a process of proposal, negotiation and agreement between the architect and client, noting that the latter may be an individual, a committee in a design-and-build contractor or institution, another consultant or some other entity. The fee will normally be agreed at a level that is a compromise between the client's desire to pay and the architect's requirements for project costs, overheads and profit.

In the past architects' fees followed a mandatory minimum fee scale based on percentages of construction costs for different types of buildings, but in 1982 this process was stopped [note 1] and at the time of writing fees are purely a matter of mutual agreement between the architect and client.

It is particularly important when proposing and agreeing fees that the architect understands how much it will really cost his or her practice to carry out the project to ensure that the fees will adequately cover the costs, with overheads, of the work to be carried out. The figure should allow the architect sufficient resources to competently complete the tasks allocated in the contract, and to fulfil their legal obligations under planning, Building Regulations and other legislation.

More information on this topic is available in the RIBA Good Practice Guide: Fees [1].

There are three common bases on which fees are agreed:

(a) percentage of the construction cost;
(b) time charge; and
(c) fixed sum fee.

(a) Percentage of the construction cost

There are surveys of fee levels published from time to time, for example by the Fees Bureau [2], but the RIBA does not publish advice on what percentages it considers to be applicable to various types of projects as categorised by use and size. The appropriate fee when calculated as a percentage of construction cost can be best assessed by applying experience gained from similar projects, or it can be determined against

Note 1 The RIBA mandatory minimum fees scale abolished in 1982 indicated fees ranging from 5% of construction cost to 11.5%. There were five categories of building types from simple, with lower fees, to more complicated with higher fees, and a sliding scale of fees for the five categories related to their size with the fee percentage reducing as the building increased in size. The abolition of this mandatory minimum scale has generally led to a reduction in fee levels.

a detailed analysis of the time and overheads that will be required to carry the work through to completion. Percentage fees are quite a crude method for calculating the money for a project, so the authors would recommend checking a fee calculated in this way against a fee proposal built up in detail from the tasks involved.

Two house projects, for example, may appear generally similar, so it might be thought that the same percentage fee would be applicable, however if one has a more complicated site it may need a more bespoke design with no repetitive elements and therefore involve more time to design and build.

If this method of calculation of fees is used, then the contract agreement should state that the fee percentage will remain constant if the construction cost increases, in other words the fee will increase as the cost of construction of the building rises. Many clients are instinctively suspicious of such arrangements as they see them as giving architects an incentive to design a more expensive building. The author's experience is that such conduct is rare within our profession, and most architects can be relied upon to work very hard to manage projects within approved budgets. It is critical however that great care is taken at the outset to establish budgets that are viable in terms of the scale, risk and complexity of any given project and site.

For this method of calculation to be viable there needs to be a realistic estimate of the building construction cost available at the stage when the architect's fees are being negotiated, however if the architect is taken on before there is any idea of what the building is like there will not be a building cost yet. For this reason architects fees are sometimes agreed on a different basis for the early stages of design then fixed into a percentage of the construction cost when there is enough design work completed to allow a reasonable cost estimate to be produced. The early design stage fees may be a time charge or a separate fixed sum.

(b) Time charge

Some clients request that the architect's work be charged solely on the basis of the time spent. If this is the case, the hourly rates should be constructed to include and cover all the required overhead and profit: Table 7.2 presents a typical example calculation of staff charge-out rates:

Time charge fees are particularly appropriate for work where the amount of time required is not known; for example, the early phases of projects before the size and shape of the building is established are often charged in this way. Some clients will be suspicious of work on a time charge thinking it gives their architect no incentive to be efficient with their time, though the author's experience is that architects are generally sensible with this. To allay this suspicion a cap can be put on the time charge work. Obviously, all hours on a project will need to be fully recorded to allow them to be invoiced.

(c) Fixed sum fee

This is the arrangement in which a fixed figure is negotiated for the work. Many clients, and some architects, prefer to have the fee for architectural and other design services fixed as it gives them certainty on the fees part of the costs of their construction project. However the architect is taking a risk because, in fixing their fee, they are being expected to absorb the cost of changes that might arise through the course of the project, and therefore the scope of work needs to be fully defined and agreed.

The basis for a fixed fee must be the most detailed calculation possible of the cost of carrying out the work built up task by task. Experience will guide the architect in knowing how much time it will take to carry out and complete the many tasks involved. The more detail that can be used in the calculation of the fee to be proposed, the more it has the likelihood of being right. Fixed sum fees are therefore more appropriate for work where the principal parameters of the project can be properly established. At a minimum these will include the following: the project brief and site; the construction cost; the construction contract type and tendering arrangement; that is, traditional, design-and-build or management, single or two-stage tender, see Chapter 12 Building contracts; and the overall project programme including the construction period.

There will however be some level of risk of additional work so a contingency should be added to the fee for this risk. Additional work can result from different causes, some examples are:

- Planning. The project taking longer to be approved through the planning process than expected.
- Tendering. The tender process taking longer than expected due to the returned prices being higher than expected, then resulting in the need to redesign some part of the project.
- Design. The design process taking longer than expected to achieve a result that meets the client's requirements.
- Third party input. If the project involves input from tenants, caterers, specialist designers and similar, their input may result in change or delay.

Table 7.2 Calculation of the overhead and profit on staff costs. The overhead figure is built up of all the office costs and includes non-productive time. VAT may need to be added to the charge-out rate where relevant.

Item		£	Total £
Person's pay per day		180.00	180.00
Individual staff costs additional to pay: holiday, pension, national insurance, etc.	Est 23%	41.40	221.40
Overheads as a percentage of staff costs	Est 100%	221.40	442.80
Profit as a percentage of staff costs plus overheads	Est 50%	221.40	664.20
Charge-out rate:			664.20

The best way for these risks to be dealt with is for the architect's appointment to allow him or her to claim additional fees when the work or the programme changes. If this is not the case then the architect should make a contingency allowance in the initial fee for the risk of change. This will be a judgement of the possible amount of additional work, the risk of it happening and the architect's appetite for absorbing the risks.

This contingency in the calculation of the architect's fees is unrelated to any contingency on the project construction budget. It should cover staff time, overheads, expenses and profit, and it can be reduced as the project proceeds and the risk of change reduces.

Some projects clearly cannot be costed in detail if there is unknown information, for example work to existing buildings or on sites where the site conditions are not fully known. For these a mechanism in the architect's appointment should allow for potential change, for example the final price can agreed after the existing building has been fully surveyed, or the architect can claim for additional work as the extent of it becomes clear.

Once the time taken has been calculated for all the tasks, staff can be allocated to each task and a total cost calculated. See Table 7.3 for a typical fee calculation for stages 1 and 2 of a project.

Before a fee spreadsheet of the kind shown in Table 7.3 can be assembled, the project tasks should be programmed out and staff allocated to them (see Chapter 6 People management Table 6.1). This is a simplified spreadsheet showing the principles that will also be applicable on a larger scale for a major project.

The RIBA offers an online fee calculator for registered members which builds up a fee task by task from time charge rates including all overheads and profit [3]. In Chapter 14 Computing, Management and accounts systems, we discuss software packages that can be used for the calculation of the fees for a project, and when the project is won, they can be used to monitor the profitability of the work as it progresses.

The Fees Bureau survey for 2024 shows the following as a typical split of fees across the RIBA stages:

RIBA stage 1: 5%
RIBA stage 2: 15%
RIBA stage 3: 18%
RIBA stage 4: 32%
RIBA stage 5: 26%
RIBA stage 6: 4%
Total: 100%

If the fees can be 'front end loaded', that is, more money charged for the early stages of the project, then the finances of the project will be cash positive through the period of design and construction.

Competitive tendering

If the architect finds him- or herself in a competitive fee tender, they should be alert for the risk of tendering too low as they do not want to find themselves in the position of not having the required budgeted staff to complete the work. The architect has a duty to make a proper provision for fees against all services that experience tells him or her will be needed or are set out in the appointment, see the ARB The Architects Code: Standard of Professional Conduct and Practice, Manage your business competently [4]. In giving their offer the architect should be precise about what is included and what not included so that additional fees can be claimed for elements outside of the bid fee.

VAT

VAT is sometimes not shown on fee proposals and just referred to with a note saying, 'fees quoted ex VAT'. Do not forget to indicate the basis on which the fees are set out – with or

Table 7.3 Typical fee calculation for a fixed sum fee for RIBA stages 1 and 2 of a project

Programme	Salary (annual)	Adjusted salary (x 1.23)	Weekly (/54)	Week 1	Week 2	Week 3	Week 4	Week 5	Week 6	TOTAL
RIBA 1 Preparation and brief										
RIBA 2 Concept design										
Staff										
Person				Staff utilisation						
Xavier	50,000.00	61,500.00	1,138.89	50%	50%	50%	50%	50%	100%	
Yasmine	35,000.00	43,050.00	797.22	75%	75%	75%	75%	75%	75%	
Zachary	25,000.00	30,750.00	569.44	100%	100%	100%	100%	100%	100%	
Sub-total				1,736.81	1,736.81	1,736.81	1,736.81	1,736.81	2,306.25	10,990.28
Overheads										
Rate		100%		1,736.81	1,736.81	1,736.81	1,736.81	1,736.81	2,306.25	
Sub-total staff plus overhead				3,473.61	3,473.61	3,473.61	3,473.61	3,473.61	4,612.50	21,980.56
Profit										
Rate		50%		1,736.81	1,736.81	1,736.81	1,736.81	1,736.81	2,306.25	
Sub-total: staff, overhead plus profit				5,210.42	5,210.42	5,210.42	5,210.42	5,210.42	6,918.75	
Expenses										
Travel				100.00		100.00				
Model									10,000.00	
Sub-total of expenses				100.00		100.00			10,000.00	10,200.00
Mark-up on expenses		10%		10.00		10.00			1,000.00	
Expenses including mark-up				110.00		110.00			11,000.00	
TOTAL (staff plus overhead, profit and expenses)				**5,320.42**	**5,210.42**	**5,320.42**	**5,210.42**	**5,210.42**	**17,918.75**	**44,190.83**
VAT Rate		20%		1,064.08	1,042.08	1,064.08	1,042.08	1,042.08	3,583.75	8,838.17
TOTAL including VAT				6,384.50	6,252.50	6,384.50	6,252.50	6,252.50	21,502.50	53,029.00
Total fee by RIBA stages					**10,530.83**				**33,660.00**	
Total fee by RIBA stages including VAT					12,637.00				40,392.00	

without VAT – as there are instances of architects forgetting to indicate that their agreed fee did not include it and ending up paying the VAT themselves out of their income.

Inflation

For projects extending over more than one year, a realistic estimated inflation figure should be included.

Invoicing

Clients will not pay unless they receive an invoice. The appointment for each project should set out the invoicing, see Chapter 9 Project delivery. Before submitting an invoice, contact the client to confirm they are expecting it and to understand their invoicing process.

An invoice should include:

The date of issue;
The name of the client;
Name and address of the practice submitting the invoice;
The agreement under which the invoice is issued;
The period for which the invoice is issued;
If the invoice is part of a total amount, the figure previously invoiced;
The amount of the invoice separately showing the net, VAT and gross cost where relevant;
The bank account details to which the money should be transferred or other process of payments accepted. Some accounts software packages can include a payment link on an invoice issued by the software;
The practice VAT number;
The due date when payment is expected.

Note that on an 'accruals basis' HMRC will require to be paid the VAT when an invoice is issued, not when the invoice is paid. To avoid the cash-flow implications of this a pro forma invoice can potentially be issued to the client first, effectively an advice note, and when they pay this the VAT invoice can then be issued. Some clients will not accept this arrangement and it may also delay the payments to the architect. The author would advise that you seek professional advice from your accountant on this area.

Chasing payment (credit control)

If invoices are not paid, a process should be followed to obtain payment:

- Issue a statement of outstanding accounts. This should be issued soon after the payment is due.
- Contact the client to find out why payment is delayed. This should be an agreed escalating series of contacts to an agreed timescale, with the accounts department probably first, and the senior partner ringing the senior client last. The timing of different contacts will be a judgement depending on how concerned the practice is about the client. Note that payments can be delayed for many reasons from slow bureaucracy to intentional non-payment and no judgement should be made on this until the reason is known.
- After an agreed period send a letter saying that legal proceedings will be commencing in seven days.
- Commence legal proceedings. Note that professional indemnity insurers may want prior notice of the intention to take legal proceedings for fee recovery, as such proceedings may illicit a counter claim by the client for non-performance of work. Some insurance policies cover for the cost of legal action to recover fees. Legal action against a client is likely to damage the relationship with them, so it should be carefully considered before starting.

Sub-consultants

The other design consultants on the project may be appointed separately to the client or the client may ask that they are appointed as sub-consultants to the architect. In either case, all the costs of all the sub-consultants must be included at proposal stage. If the architect finds he or she needs additional sub-consultants after the project appointment is signed, their costs are likely to come out of the architect's overall fees. The sub-consultants should be appointed and paid on the same basis as the architect with the same programme, similar contract terms and a similar basis of payment.

Pay-when-paid

Note that in the UK it is not legal to appoint sub-consultants on a basis that they will only be paid after the architect is paid. Therefore an allowance may have to be made in the project finances and cashflows for the payment of sub-consultants before receipt of payment from the client.

The total project fee will be the sum of all the fees for the architect plus all the other consultants required on the project. Table 7.4 shows a typical calculation of the total fee for a project based on the RIBA stages.

Ongoing project cost control

Once the appointment is signed and the architect starts their work on a project the finances should be reviewed monthly to compare how much has been spent with what was predicted. This should be discussed within the practice, and the whole project team, so that staffing or the working method can be adjusted if required to keep a financial position that is acceptable to the company.

The work completed on the project should be assessed in parallel with how much fee has been spent, the primary project

Table 7.4 A typical overall project fee calculation

RIBA stages	1	2	3	4	5	6	Total
Fees including expenses	5%	10%	20%	35%	25%	5%	100%
Architect and principal designer	10,531	33,660	58,921	1,03,112	73,651	14,730	2,94,606
Structural and civil engineer	4,212	13,464	23,568	41,245	29,461	5,892	1,17,842
Services engineer	4,212	13,464	23,568	41,245	29,461	5,892	1,17,842
Landscape designer	1,580	5,049	8,838	15,467	11,048	2,210	44,191
Planning consultant	2,106	6,732	11,784	1,547	1,105	221	23,495
Quantity surveyor	2,106	6,732	11,784	20,622	14,730	2,946	58,921
TOTAL	**24,747**	**79,101**	**1,38,465**	**2,23,237**	**1,59,455**	**31,891**	**6,56,897**
VAT at 20%	4,949	15,820	27,693	44,647	31,891	6,378	1,31,379
Total including VAT	29,697	94,921	1,66,158	2,67,885	1,91,346	38,269	7,88,276

expenditure normally being staff costs. If more money has been spent than intended, then corrective action will need to be taken: if for example 50% of the allocated staff time has been used up, but only 25% of the design work or production drawings have been completed, then corrective action, where possible, will be required. It is better in these circumstances to review the work to be completed against the remaining fees to develop a plan of how to finish the work within the hours available.

If the project is costing more than expected and the fee is a fixed sum, then it may be possible to take corrective action to reduce expenditure so that the amount spent will be less than the fee by the completion of the work. Such action might be to reduce costs, for example by allocating more work to junior staff or by changing a working method so that a task is completed in less time or with fewer staff or it might be that the team will have to work unpaid overtime to complete the work that should have been done. The earlier this corrective action is taken the more likely it is to succeed.

In Chapter 14 Computing, Management and accounts systems, we discuss software packages that can be used to monitor the profitability of the work as it progresses.

References

[1] Farrall, P. and Brookhouse, S. 2021. *Good Practice Guide: Fees.* London: RIBA Publishing.
[2] The Fees Bureau. https://thefeesbureau.co.uk/architects
[3] RIBA Fee Calculator. https://www.architecture.com/digital-practice-tools/riba-fee-calculator
[4] https://arb.org.uk/wp-content/uploads/2016/05/Architects-Code-2017.pdf

8
Environmental sustainability

Introduction

The purpose of environmental sustainability is to look after the planet so that we can hand it on to the next generation in a decent state. This will involve all of us doing our part, including those of us running an architecture practice.

Sustainability is a word that is also used in other contexts where sometimes people talk about economic and social sustainability, however in this chapter we are discussing the natural environment, how to reduce deleterious impacts on it and have beneficial effects on the world, that is, environmental sustainability.

The environmental sustainability policy

RIBA Chartered Practices are required to have an environmental management policy and the RIBA has an Environmental Management Policy Guide for them which includes a template environmental policy.

Larger practices can achieve compliance with ISO 14001 2015 Environmental Management Systems – Requirements with guidance for use. This standard specifies the requirements for an environmental management system that an organisation can use to enhance its environmental performance.

Practices can also buy external certification to confirm their compliance with this standard which can be audited annually and the certificate renewed at longer intervals.

To ensure the environmental sustainability policy is implemented as intended, the practice should identify individuals

DOI: 10.4324/9781003327288-10

responsible for the different activities and nominate a person to regularly check its implementation and to review the policy.

Like other policies, an environmental sustainability policy should be regularly reviewed and updated to reconfirm the aims, incorporate new thinking on the subject, and to take account of changes in the office such as changes to the premises or design software.

Communications

The environmental policy of the office needs the buy-in of everyone in the practice and should be part of the overall culture of the company. The policy should be communicated to everyone in the office so that they can play their part.

The environmental policy also needs to be communicated outside the practice. It should ensure that a range of environmental objectives that could inform the design process are communicated to other parties at the appropriate time – that is to clients, contractors, other consultants, local authorities and so forth. This will help to bring environmental policy aims into the discussion so that they can be adopted into projects.

The sustainable office

There are various ways an architect's office can reduce its environmental impact:

Occupy a sustainably designed building. The practice can set an example by occupying a building that has a low overall impact on the environment over its whole lifetime – that has a low carbon input in construction, has low energy use in operation and can be recycled when demolished. The office should also be located to allow staff and visitors to travel there by public transport or by bicycle.

Reduce the use of non-renewable energy. As with any other building the heating, lighting and power of the practice office can be from renewable sources. The reduction in the quantity of energy used is also part of the picture of reducing the overall environmental impact of the building.

Reduce waste. The office can reduce the amount of waste it produces in its day-to-day operations and ensure any waste is recycled.

Avoid materials that are harmful to the environment or hazardous to humans. Materials or products that are known to be detrimental to the environment can be avoided or reduced. If any products in the office are harmful to health the office may be required to make a health and safety assessment under the Control of Substances Hazardous to Health (COSHH) regulations 2002 [1]. This may include chemicals, wood dust, fumes, certain plants and food processes. Measures can be taken to counteract the impacts from these.

Reduce the impact of travel. If you are designing projects around the country and around the world this will involve travelling to sites and meetings, which should be done in the most sustainable way possible – cycling or taking public transport in preference to using a car, taking a train in preference to flying and holding meetings by video call in preference to travelling at all.

Environmental sustainability of projects

The design of buildings to reduce their environmental impact or even to have a net positive effect is a large topic that is well discussed in other publications. We describe here the major environmental assessment, certification and accreditation schemes.

BREEAM

Building Research Establishment Environmental Assessment Method run by the UK Building Research Establishment [2] is a voluntary, that is not mandatory, scheme for the rating of construction projects against a set of criteria. The criteria are organised for different types of buildings:

- UK new construction;
- Infrastructure;
- International new construction;
- UK refurbishment and fit-out;
- International refurbishment and fit-out;
- UK domestic refurbishment.

And if a building doesn't fit into any of these categories a bespoke rating process can be followed in consultation with BREEAM.

The project wins credits for achieving targets described within a detailed list constructed against the following topics:

management, health and wellbeing; energy; transport; water; materials; waste; land use and ecology; pollution; innovation.

Some of the targets require action from the very beginning of the project, others during design and during construction, though the final rating will be given on completion of the building.

The credits earned are used to calculate a final percentage rating and a classification. Table 8.1 lists the BREEAM ratings.

Table 8.1 BREEAM ratings of buildings

BREEAM rating	% score
Outstanding	≥ 85
Excellent	≥ 70
Very good	≥ 55
Good	≥ 45
Pass	≥ 30
Unclassified	< 30

The rating is awarded by an independent BREEAM assessor who should be appointed at the beginning of the project. The assessor will charge a fee. Evidence will need to be presented to them to prove the stated targets have been achieved, and evidence may need to be collected from day one of RIBA stage 1.

LEED

Leadership in Energy and Environmental Design, run by the US Green Building Council [3], is a voluntary scheme which is intended to rate the environmental performance of projects.

The project must be registered, a fee paid and an application submitted which is then reviewed by Green Business Certification Incorporated, who will issue the certification if the building achieves sufficient credits.

The project can be rated under classifications:

- Building design and construction;
- Interior design and construction;
- Operation and maintenance;
- Cities;
- Communities.

Under each of these headings are then a list of building or project types.

The credits that can be won are under a list of topics. By way of example the following headings apply to the category Building Design and Construction:

- Commercial: integrative process;
- Location and transportation;
- Sustainable sites, water efficiency;
- Energy and atmosphere;
- Materials and resources;
- Indoor environmental quality;

- Innovation;
- Regional priority.

The number of credits that a project achieved will establish the overall LEED rating that is awarded. These are listed in Table 8.2.

Other similar rating schemes

Other similar rating schemes around the world include:

Green Star in Australia [4];
HQE in France, Haute Qualité Environnementale, run by the Association pour la Haute Qualité Environnementale [5].

Passivhaus

Passivhaus is a voluntary standard for construction of low-carbon buildings developed primarily in Germany and managed in the UK by the Passivhaus Trust [6], an affiliate of the International Passive House Association (iPHA). It was originally applied to houses but has subsequently been adopted for housing, offices, educational buildings and refurbishments. It consists of a set of design criteria that, if achieved, will result in a building that requires very little energy in use. A registered Passivhaus Certifier can be engaged to assess the project, noting that the assessment work for certification work starts normally at the design stage.

Table 8.2 The LEED ratings

LEED rating	Number of points achieved
Platinum	80 and above
Gold	60 to 79
Silver	50 to 59
Certified	40 to 49

To assess a design against the Passivhaus standard a project should be modelled at an early stage using the Passive House Planning Package, it should be designed and built following the Passivhaus recommendations, and it should pass a series of tests on completion. It will then be certified under one of three categories – 'classic', 'plus' or 'premium'.

Securing certification under the Passivhaus scheme requires a design and specification that offers:

• Very high levels of insulation within the external envelope including to the ground;
• Extremely high performance windows with well-insulated frames;
• Airtight building fabric;
• 'Thermal bridge free' construction;
• A mechanical ventilation system with highly efficient heat recovery.

These requirements, if met, will result in low energy consumption and a comfortable environment for users of the building.

Other standards

There are other standards that building designers and users can follow to promote environmental sustainability, for example ISO 20121, Sustainable Event Management and ISO 14001, 2015 TC, Environmental management systems, Requirements with guidance for use. The Code for Sustainable Homes was introduced in 2006 and withdrawn in 2015 when its provisions were incorporated into the Building Regulations, and is sometimes still referred to.

References

[1] COSHH: Control of Substances Hazardous to Health Regulations 2002 (as amended in 2004) – General Enforcement Guidance and Advice – OC 273/20. hse.gov.uk

[2] BREEAM. https://bregroup.com/products/breeam/how-breeam-works/

[3] US Green Building Council. https://www.usgbc.org

[4] Green Building Council of Australia. https://new.gbca.org.au/green-star/exploring-green-star/),

[5] French Association Pour la Haute Qualité Environnementale. https://www.hqegbc.org

[6] The Passivhaus Trust. https://www.passivhaustrust.org.uk

Project management

9
Project delivery

Introduction

This chapter uses the RIBA Plan of Work (Figure 9.1) as the basis for a description of the work involved through the stages of a design and construction project. We use the RIBA Plan of Work as it is a widely accepted industry standard for the phases of a project. Note that this plan of work is regularly updated, so the latest version should be referred to [1].

The RIBA Plan of Work

The RIBA Plan of Work is a guide to the activities a design team will carry out through the life of a project designing and constructing a building. It is a useful guide and easy reference referred to by all participants in the construction industry. The current version has been written to reflect the latest industry practice including procurement, planning, modern methods of construction and sustainability.

The reader will note that the Plan of Work has a series of sections setting out the work to be done in each stage:

Stage outcome:	The main items of work to be achieved in the stage.
Core tasks:	The main tasks to be completed to achieve the stage outcome.
Core statutory processes:	The planning and building regulations tasks per stage.

DOI: 10.4324/9781003327288-12

Figure 9.1 The RIBA Plan of Work 2020

Source: Note this plan of work is regularly updated and the latest version should be referred to [1]. The RIBA Plan of Work has been reproduced with permission of the RIBA.

3	4	5	6	7
Spatial Coordination	**Technical Design**	**Manufacturing and Construction**	**Handover**	**Use**
outcome of Stage 0 may be the decision to initiate a project and Stage 7 covers the ongoing use of the building. ------>				
Architectural and engineering information **Spatially Coordinated**	All design information required to manufacture and construct the project completed	Manufacturing, construction and **Commissioning** completed	Building handed over, **Aftercare** initiated and **Building Contract** concluded	Building used, operated and maintained efficiently
	Stage 4 will overlap with Stage 5 on most projects	There is no design work in Stage 5 other than responding to **Site Queries**		Stage 7 starts concurrently with Stage 6 and lasts for the life of the building
Undertake **Design Studies, Engineering Analysis** and **Cost Exercises** to test **Architectural Concept** resulting in **Spatially Coordinated** design aligned to updated **Cost Plan, Project Strategies** and **Outline Specification** Initiate **Change Control Procedures** Prepare stage **Design Programme**	Develop architectural and engineering technical design Prepare and coordinate design team **Building Systems** information Prepare and integrate specialist subcontractor **Building Systems** information Prepare stage **Design Programme**	Finalise **Site Logistics** Manufacture **Building Systems** and construct building Monitor progress against **Construction Programme** Inspect **Construction Quality** Resolve **Site Queries** as required Undertake **Commissioning** of building Prepare **Building Manual**	Hand over building in line with **Plan for Use Strategy** Undertake review of **Project Performance** Undertake seasonal **Commissioning** Rectify defects Complete initial **Aftercare** tasks including light touch **Post Occupancy Evaluation**	Implement **Facilities Management** and **Asset Management** Undertake **Post Occupancy Evaluation** of building performance in use Verify **Project Outcomes** including **Sustainability Outcomes**
	Specialist subcontractor designs are prepared and reviewed during Stage 4	Building handover tasks bridge Stages 5 and 6 as set out in the **Plan for Use Strategy**		Adaptation of a building (at the end of its useful life) triggers a new Stage 0
Review design against **Building Regulations** Prepare and submit **Planning Application**	Submit **Building Regulations Application** Discharge pre-commencement **Planning Conditions** Prepare **Construction Phase Plan** Submit form F10 to HSE if applicable	Carry out **Construction Phase Plan** Comply with **Planning Conditions** related to construction	Comply with **Planning Conditions** as required	Comply with **Planning Conditions** as required
See **Planning Note** for guidance on submitting a **Planning Application** earlier than at end of Stage 3				
	Tender / Appoint contractor			
	ER CP — Appoint contractor			
Pre-contract services agreement	CP — Appoint contractor			Appoint **Facilities Management** and **Asset Management** teams, and strategic advisers as needed
Preferred bidder	CP — Appoint contractor			
Signed off **Stage Report** **Project Strategies** Updated **Outline Specification** Updated **Cost Plan** **Planning Application**	**Manufacturing Information** **Construction Information** **Final Specifications** Residual **Project Strategies** **Building Regulations Application**	**Building Manual** including Health and Safety File and Fire Safety Information **Practical Completion** certificate including Defects List **Asset Information**	Feedback on **Project Performance** **Final Certificate** Feedback from light touch **Post Occupancy Evaluation**	Feedback from **Post Occupancy Evaluation** Updated **Building Manual** including Health and Safety File and Fire Safety Information as necessary
		If **Verified Construction Information** is required, verification tasks must be defined		

Further guidance and detailed stage descriptions are included in the RIBA Plan of Work 2020 Overview.

© RIBA 2020

| Procurement route: | The tasks to be carried out related to tendering and appointing a contractor. |
| Information exchanges: | The main items of information to be issued by the architect or procured by them from others. |

The RIBA then publishes other documents to assist with using the Plan of Work:

- Plan of Work Overview. A leaflet to expand the Plan of Work and to help the architect understand and use it.
- Plan of Work Toolbox. An Excel spreadsheet to be filled in by the user with the tasks to be undertaken per stage for their own project.
- Design for Manufacture and Assembly Overlay. A leaflet containing additional tasks for design and issue of information for off-site manufacture of elements and assemblies.
- Security Overlay. A leaflet issued by the RIBA with the National Protective Security Authority containing additional tasks related to designing a building to be more resistant to vandalism, theft and terrorism.
- Inclusive Design Overlay. A leaflet including tasks to achieve a design accessible to all.
- Engagement Overlay. A leaflet setting out tasks for incorporating broader participation of interest groups and the wider public in the design process.
- Smart Building Overlay. A leaflet including additional tasks for designers of buildings with additional technology for monitoring and controlling the building systems.

We let the reader look at the RIBA plan to see the tasks he or she may be asked to carry out at each phase. This chapter gives commentary on the tasks and guidance on how to manage them.

The RIBA Job Book [2] which accompanies the Plan of Work lists out tasks and advice for each stage of a project in more detail than is described here and includes standard forms and letters.

Architects will sometimes hear people in the industry refer to the old RIBA Plan of Work phases, which go by letters rather than numbers. This was last published in 2007 and was replaced by the current version in 2013.

Many countries have their own model for the phases of a project, certainly all the major European countries do, and the American Institute of Architects has one. Table 9.1 shows a comparison of some of these with the RIBA Plan of Work. If an architect is working outside the UK, or for a client from outside the UK, and they are asked to follow other phase names, the architect is advised to go to the current original version of the plan of work being referenced to ensure they have understood correctly what the phases consist of, what are the deliverables, and how to use the plan.

The architect's appointment

In Chapter 5 Marketing and business development we discuss winning a project. In Chapter 7 Finances we discuss project fees. Once the architect is awarded a project an appointment must be signed, after the terms have been agreed.

The RIBA Code of Professional Conduct, principle 2 Competence, paragraph 2.1 says: 'All terms of appointment between a Member and their client must be clear, agreed and recorded in writing before the commencement of any professional services'. The ARB's The Architects Code: Standards of Professional Conduct and Practice[1] has similar requirements.

The architect is recommended to use the RIBA Professional Services Contract [3], which is the UK industry standard architect's appointment with a balanced relationship between architect

Table 9.1 RIBA 2022 Plan of Work overview comparing plan of work stages from some other countries.

Country or organisation	Pre-design 0	1	Design 2	3	4		Construction 5	Handover 6	In use 7
RIBA (UK)	Strategic definition	Preparation and briefing	Concept design	Spatial coordination	Technical design		Manufacturing and construction	Handover	In use
AIA (Aus) Contract services		B.1 Feasibility Study	A.1 Concept Design	A.2 Design Development	A.4 Construction Documents	A.5 Contractor Selection	A.6 Construction Administration	B2. Record Documents	
OA (France)	OAD Administrative preparation	PROG Brief	APS Concept	APD Developed design	PCG & MDT Project design & construction documents		DET & VISA Construction phase and comment on contractor's submittals	AOR Handover	
HOAI (Germany)	LP1 Strategic definition	LP2 Preparation and briefing	LP3 Conceptual design	LP4 Planning application	LP5 Technical design	LP6 & LP7 Technical design for tender and tender award	LP8 Construction	LP9 Handover	
AIA (USA)	PR Pre-design		SD Schematic design	DD Design development	CD Construction documents	BP & BN Building permit and bidding and negotiating	CA Construction administration		

Note: The stages and the scope of work in each stage do not align exactly between different countries. The reader should refer to the plan of work for each country to get full information.

and client and well-resolved provisions. There is a standard version, and then versions for the following:

- Interior design;
- Conservation work;
- Domestic projects;
- Principal designer;
- Client adviser;
- Sub-consultant; and
- Concise forms.

The architect may, however, be appointed by means of a letter exchanged between them and the client, or by a bespoke contract written for the project.

Any bespoke contract offered by a client should be studied carefully to ensure it includes everything required and that the architect agrees with all the terms suggested. The author of such a contract, probably a lawyer acting for the client, is likely to draft the contents to favour their client, and the architect may need to negotiate terms that leave them in no worse a position than if they had used the standard form of appointment. Some terms that might be proposed are:

- Amendment of the standard of care to be used by the architect;
- Extension of the scope of work into areas the architect may not be willing or able to perform;
- Inclusion of guarantees or indemnities.

If the standard of care is greater than 'reasonable skill and care', for example if the architect is proposed to 'ensure' performance, this may fall outside the architect's professional indemnity insurance. Similarly guarantees or indemnities should be avoided as they are likely to be outside the PII cover.

Further information on contracts is available in the *Architect's Legal Handbook* [4] or the *Architect's Legal Pocket Book* [5], and if the architect is unsure how to proceed they should seek legal advice. Items that affect the architect's PI insurance should be discussed with the insurer.

Any contract should include the following, and worth noting that it is an ARB requirement that certain topics are included, such as:

- The contracting parties;
- An outline description of the project;
- The architect's scope of work including important pro-gramme dates such as commencement and completion. This should include a mechanism for agreeing changes if required;
- The architect's fee or method of calculating it. The timing and amount of each invoice. This should include a mecha-nism for adjustments to the fee in response to changes in the scope or programme;
- Who will be responsible for what;
- Any limitations on the responsibilities of the parties;
- The architect's responsibility to use 'reasonable skill and care' in performance of the services;
- Provisions for suspension or termination of the agreement, including any legal rights of cancellation;
- Confirmation that the architect has insurance. The architect is recommended to agree as low a figure as possible for their liability and less than the limit of their insurance;
- The architect's retention of copyright of their work;
- A method for resolving disputes;
- That the architect is registered with the ARB and subject to its Code.

Alongside the normal core architectural design duties the architect may be appointed as:

- Lead designer – a role leading the design work of the other design consultants;

- Lead consultant – a role leading the design work and managing the other consultants. This is a role described in the 'services' section of the RIBA Standard Professional Services Contract 2020;
- Project lead or project manager – a role managing all aspects of the project. This is a role described in the 'services' section of the RIBA Standard Professional Services Contract 2020;
- Contract administrator – a specific role identified in the JCT Standard Building Contract with various duties to administer the contract;
- Principal Designer is a defined term in the CDM regulations and Building Safety Act;
- Client adviser – primarily a role advising the client in a project where there is a design-and-build contractor employing their own design team.

These may be identified as separate roles, or they may be incorporated into the architect's scope of work without being named.

Termination

The RIBA Standard Professional Services Contract includes a right for both the client and the architect to terminate the contract under certain circumstances. Sometimes a contract may be offered to the architect that includes a right for termination by the client only and the architect should ensure that their right to terminate should be included.

There is a risk to the architect if their work is suspended on a project, or they are just not instructed to do any work, but the contract is left open without being formally terminated. In this circumstance the architect may find they have contractual responsibility without any work or fees, and they should therefore ensure the contract is terminated in writing. The architect should always be alert to the risks associated with answering questions or being helpful when they are not appointed or being paid for their advice.

The appointment should be signed by both parties before work is commenced.

Collateral warranties

A collateral warranty is a contract that passes the architect's responsibilities to the client in their appointment on to funders or purchasers of the building or to tenants. The purpose is to allow those parties to take legal action against the architect if there is a problem with the building, and therefore collateral warranties are often requested by commercial clients. They are to be avoided, if possible, but if required they should be studied to ensure they do not create greater liability than in the main appointment.

The document should preserve the architect's right to seek contributions towards the cost of a claim from the other consultants which they would have under the main appointment. If the other consultants have not signed a collateral warranty, a clause should be inserted stating the architect is only liable to the extent of their part in the design of the building, called a 'net contribution' clause. PI insurance is only likely to pay to the extent the architect was liable for the problem anyway. The architect should also ensure the liability is not able to be passed on further than the named party in the collateral warranty.

Sub-consultants

If the architect is employing sub-consultants to carry out part of their scope of work, the sub-consultancy agreement should preferably be the standard RIBA form listed previously, and its terms should always be back to back with the architect's appointment. Note however that it is not legal to appoint sub-consultants in the UK on a pay-when-paid basis.

General principles of project communications

For a project to run smoothly and with the minimum of risk to all the parties involved, a level of formality and efficiency is required in the working processes. The author recommends:

Communicate fully: people need to know what is going on, so more communication is better than less.

Communicate to everyone: some people who are not directly involved with a particular topic will benefit from knowing about a subject as it may inform their work indirectly, though conversely everyone should not be copied in to every email so that their inboxes are not overloaded.

Communications should be in writing: there must be a full record of the actions and decisions on the project so that anyone can track back to find out what happened, when and why. Only written evidence can be produced in a future legal dispute.

Communications should be timely. People are working on design or construction, so if some piece of information affects their work they deserve to know as soon as possible to avoid wasting time and money.

Project meetings

The following meetings are common during the design stages of a project. The meetings will be different during the construction stages:

Client meeting

Between the client and his or her consultants. This should be chaired and minuted by the architect, though if there is a project manager or client's representative on the project they may perform these roles. This is the regular forum for the design team to keep the client appraised of progress on the design and for them to get the client's comments and decisions on any matters arising. There may be separate design presentations and workshops for more in-depth discussions.

Project team meeting

Between all the consultant team. This should be led and minuted by the architect. The purpose is to communicate between the team, reporting on progress, monitoring the programme and coordinating between the consultants.

Meetings with the local authority building regulations team

Again these should be led and minuted by the architect. On smaller projects there may be only one meeting, or none at all, whilst for larger and more complicated buildings a weekly meeting may be required. The purpose is to discuss the regulatory aspects of the design and thereby to ensure the project complies with the regulations before being formally submitted for approval, and to discuss and resolve any conditions on the building regulations approval.

Local residents' or stakeholders' meeting

To bring the local community on side with a project – the earlier they are part of the project process the better. The client and design team can decide how influential they want the residents to be depending on the type of project. If the project is housing, then it is valuable to consult the people who will live there; for a commercial building in a commercial district the neighbouring tenants will not expect to have so much influence.

Project set-up

The timing of the architect's appointment

The appointment of the architect may occur at any time from stage 0 Strategic Definition to stage 4 Technical Design (when another practice has done the initial stages of design), and at whichever stage the architect is appointed they will need to carry out a process of project set-up when they start. This section describes the tasks at the beginning of the project.

The RIBA Plan of Work describes the tasks to be done at each stage in outline, but there is no clear definition of the deliverables at each stage. This can lead to misunderstandings about the work being done by the architect and other members of the design team unless it is further defined project by project. For example in stage 2 Concept Design it says 'Prepare Architectural Design incorporating Strategic Engineering requirements and aligned to Cost Plan, Project Strategies and Outline Specification'. To proceed with the design work this needs to be expanded to a full set of deliverables and a design responsibility matrix, then a project programme added.

The author has produced illustrations showing the level of detail expected at stages 1 Preparation and Briefing, 2 Concept Design, 3 Spatial Coordination and 4 Technical Design for a typical small project, see Figures 9.3, 9.4, 9.5 and 9.6. These are intended as a guide to the information that might be expected based on the author's experience, however the architect should confirm the intended level of information with the client for each project.

Main project processes

Once the architect's appointment is signed the project processes need to be established at commencement of the project. There are many communication and design processes involved in a project of which some primary ones are:

- Lines of communication. One person should be identified from each party – the client, architect, engineer, quantity surveyor etc. – as the central person for issue and receipt of emails, letters and so forth. They can distribute communications or nominate others for certain topics. This mechanism will make it more likely that important information is seen by the right people and dealt with appropriately.
- The schedule of meetings listed earlier.
- The processes for the internal checking, issue, distribution and recording of drawings and reports being issued.
- The processes for receiving, distributing, reviewing and returning drawings and reports from others.
- Processes for client sign-off and subsequent change control. Once the client has signed off the design at a particular stage, any change to that design, separate from design development, should go through a change control process. This can be more or less formal depending on the client's requirements.
- Management of invoices and expenses. The process for checking, issuing and paying invoices and expenses between the consultants and the client.

These form part of the project execution plan, see also Chapter 13 Quality Assurance and Stage 1 Preparation and Briefing.

Briefing for the client and other stakeholders

The client, and people working with them, for example tenants, caterers and maintenance staff, should be introduced to the architect's team and informed about how the architect intends to approach the project. Their briefing should include:

- The project processes identified earlier;
- The intentions with regard to planning and building regulations;

- The project programme;
- The intentions with regard to procurement of a contractor;
- Information required from the client;
- The client design presentations, and then how and when a sign-off will be requested from the client.

It is helpful to inform the client and his or her team of the importance of their decision-making; that the project will run smoothly if they make the decisions requested of them within the time identified, and don't change their mind. It is then incumbent on the architect to provide to the client all the information they need in good time to enable them to make the decisions.

Appointment of all the consultants

The architect should ensure that all the other consultants the project needs are appointed either directly by the client or as sub-consultants to the architect. The first other design consultant required is a structural engineer, followed by a services engineer and a cost consultant (QS). There is a tendency for increasing specialisation in the construction industry so the architect will find more design consultants specialising in smaller areas of design, for example lighting designers, catering designers, security consultants, people movement consultants. The architect should ensure that all the work required on the project is being done by one consultant or another in the team and there are no gaps.

Deliverables list

The architect should compile a deliverables list for each project stage, as should each of the other consultants. This should describe the level of definition of the drawings and other information so that the team knows what to produce and the client understands what he or she will receive. It should describe every drawing and report as clearly as they can be before the work has begun.

It can include the BIM Level of Design, see Chapter 14 Computing.

Table 9.2 Typical deliverables list for stage 2 Concept Design for a notional project

	Project name and number	Prospect House, C21
	Document RIBA Stage Date issued Revision	Deliverables list 2 Concept Design 28 May 2024 A
i	Floor plans	1:200 scale showing layout of spaces, doors, furniture in public spaces. Notional finishes identified at this time for costing purposes.
ii	Sections, 2 number	1:200 scale showing walls and floors as zones.
iii	Elevations, N, S, E and W	1:200 scale identifying the main materials.
iv	Site layout	1:200 scale showing roads, green areas, levels, main materials.
v	Details	Most design work of details would not be produced at this stage, but if there are special or unusual elements it may be useful to complete an outline design in sufficient detail to enable the design ideas to be priced or confirmed as practical.
vi	Design report	Describing the brief as developed, the ideas behind the design, and how they respond to the brief in all its aspects. If there is any part of the brief for which the design has not yet been done, this must be said. The report should cover all the topics mentioned in the RIBA Plan of Work for this stage under each of the headings: • Stage outcome at the end of the stage, • Core tasks including architecture, engineering, costs; compliance with or derogations from the brief; project stakeholders; programme. • Core statutory processes, • Procurement route, • Information exchanges, • Environmental sustainability.
vii	Visualisations	Images of the main internal public spaces, 2 of the exterior.
viii	CDM stage report	

Design responsibility matrix

This shows which member of the team is to be responsible for each item of work: design tasks; management tasks and production of items in the deliverables list.

This matrix ensures that all the work required for the project is being done by someone on the team, and informs them that they are expected to do it.

Table 9.3 Typical design responsibility matrix for stage 2 Concept Design deliverables leading up to a planning application for a notional project.

	Project name and number	Prospect House, C21						
	Document RIBA Stage Date issued Revision	Design responsibility matrix 2 Concept Design 28 May 2024 A						
	Consultant	Architect and Principal Designer	Structural Engineer	Civil Engineer	Services Engineer	Landscape Designer	Planning Consultant	Quantity Surveyor
Item	Date							
Architectural drawings including visualisations	3 April	L						
CDM report	10 Apr	L	A	A	A	A		
Structural report	10 April		L					
Civil engineering report	10 April			L				
Services engineering report	10 April				L			
Landscape design	10 April					L		

(Continued)

Table 9.3 (Continued)

	Project name and number	Prospect House, C21					
Design and access statement	17 April	L	A	A	A	A	A
Planning report	17 April	A	A	A	A	A	L
Building cost report	17 April						L

Notes: L: the consultant leads the production of the design drawings or report and is responsible to ensure information is received from others.

A: the consultant is assisting by contributing to the report when requested to by the lead.

Project programme

When the programme is being complied each person or company identified to carry out a task should confirm the time period is correct – the programme is only as good as the commitment of the people contributing to it. Some parties contributing work and therefore part of the programme are not under the control of the project team – local authorities, utility companies and other third parties, for example. These people might advise how long their tasks may take or, if not, the person compiling the programme might have to indicate the period with the best knowledge available without confirmation from them. Everyone on the project should be made aware of the level of reliability of the dates shown.

The programme can be hand-drawn or produced in Excel, Microsoft Project (the programme illustrated is in MS Project) or a more sophisticated programming software such as Oracle Primavera P6, provided it conveys the information required. The programme should be based on the most reliable information available. If people give information to go into the programme that is not fully thought through – most importantly how long they will take to complete a task – then the whole

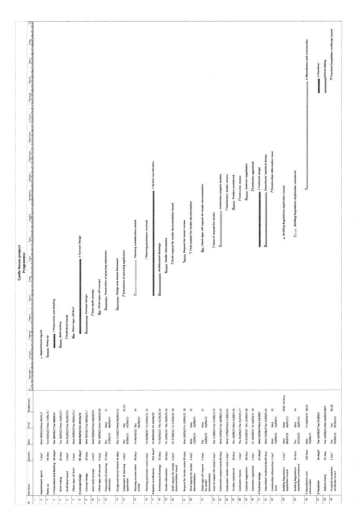

Figure 9.2 A typical outline programme for a whole project. The programme illustrated shows the typical tasks for a project

project can suffer. The timescales need to be realistic, and the individuals involved need to commit to achieving them. This includes outside consultants who have to provide information, third party stakeholders giving their input and the client making decisions.

In the programme shown in Figure 9.2 we have shown two areas where the work overlaps in ways that some clients may not be willing to accept:

- Task stage 3 Spatial Coordination (line 17) is shown running in parallel with the consideration of the planning application (line 15). Many clients ask the design team to stop work whilst they wait for the planning decision as any work done during the consideration period is at risk. If the local authority refuses the planning application or the permission is granted with major conditions any design work done on the design submitted for planning may have to be changed. On some projects however where time is critical design work can carry on in parallel with consideration of planning.

    If this overlap is not acceptable then in the programme '3 Spatial Coordination' would start after 'Planning permission received', leaving the design team inactive whilst the planning application is considered.
- Task stage 4 Technical Design (line 31) is also shown running in parallel with the tender for the main contractor (lines 25 to 30). This again creates some risk as any design development that takes place during stage 4 will have to be included in the contractor's price at the last moment of the tender. The alternative is for the tender to be issued after the end of stage 4 when the design is ready to be issued for construction, which gives greater cost certainty. On some projects however time is all important, and overlapping work as shown here is a way to reduce the overall project period.

    If this overlap is not acceptable then the tender of the main contractor would start after the end of '4 Technical Design'.

The timing of tendering of the construction contract

The construction work can be tendered from the end of stage 0 to the end of stage 4 using different types of contracts as described in Chapter 12 Building contracts and illustrated on the RIBA Plan of Work. A government agency might call for tenders at the end of stage 0 if it wants to acquire a building by design-build-and-finance tender for which it only requires the outline functional requirements. Most domestic clients are at the other end of the scale and want to control the design they are commissioning in great detail and how much it will cost – for them a tender issued at the end of stage 4 when all the design work is complete will ensure the design is what they want and the price will be unlikely to change during construction.

The architect's work will be different under a design-and-build arrangement from under a traditional contract where all the design work is completed before tender, see Chapter 12 Building contracts.

Monitoring the programme

The programme should be monitored to assess progress and updated in a cycle described as 'plan, do, review, adjust'.

The first part of the review is to assess where the work is against the programme, which should be done task by task. It can be tempting to think if you have spent two weeks on a two-week task that you have completed it, or to think if you have spent 70 labour hours on a two-week task for one person that it is complete, however this may not be true. A task should be assessed on output only – how complete are the drawings or reports to be produced? – unless it is a task without output, such as attending a meeting. Assessing the completeness of a drawing can be a matter of judgement, so if it is 90% complete, will it only take another 10% of the time to be finished, or is the last 10% the most difficult that will take 50% of the time to complete? The author's advice is that you should be rigorously realistic in assessing the completeness of work.

More sophisticated programming software including Microsoft Project and Oracle Primavera P6 have a function to update a whole programme if the operator inputs the completion percentages for all the tasks. The effect of any tasks being completed early or late will be calculated automatically through to completion.

A construction programme can have a 'critical path'. This is the series of tasks that are crucial to the project and lead through to its completion, for example the critical path might run through the waterproofing of the roof as the interiors of a building can only be started when the inside is guaranteed to be dry.

A plan of work and programme never turn out quite as expected, and the normal result of the unexpected is delay. There are many reasons why work may be later than planned, some examples include: members of the team taking longer than expected to do their work for whatever reason; the client or others taking longer than expected to make decisions, or not making decisions at all; consultants or other third parties over which the architect has less control not providing their input in the timescale expected. To allow for this a programme would logically contain an item titled 'float' or 'spare time', however this would not work as people have a tendency not to fully commit to completing their work on time if they can see some available extra time. Better for the programme to have intermediate deadlines and a final deadline that commits to deliver the information early. If the final deadline for the whole team is before the final date when the information is required, then everyone is working to the same goal and any spare time is outside the normal working targets of the team. Intermediate deadlines are a good mechanism to allow the progress of work to be partially completed and assessed before the final issue date, so that the programme, or the team, can be adjusted to cover the areas where work is behind schedule.

Other project set-up tasks

Staffing plan

Once the scope of work and programme are settled the staff can be allocated to the various tasks in a staffing plan, see Chapter 6 People management Figure 6.1.

Project cost plan (the office plan for the project)

With the deliverables, programme and staffing plan completed the project cost plan showing the office costs for the project can be adjusted to reflect the final cost of staff and overheads. See Chapter 7 Finances.

The RIBA Plan of Work stages

This section gives important thoughts and pointers about each RIBA work stage. It is not a comprehensive description of all the tasks to be done throughout a project; more comprehensive detail of the tasks at each design stage can be found in the *RIBA Job Book* [2].

Stage 0 Strategic Definition

Most often the architect is not appointed at this stage. It is when a client decides on the need for a building project then identifies the broad requirements and their budget.

The client, with their advisors, will set out what building they want, and also the process of procuring it:

The building: core project requirements, which may be a business case or functional requirements and a budget.
Sustainability aims.

A site, or maybe a site selection process if there is not one identified.

A target timescale.

The process of procuring it: who will lead the project – the client or a consultant?

The outline of the contracting method – which contracting route does the client want?

What are the risks around the project?

From these elements the building brief, procurement strategy, responsibility matrix, sustainability strategy, and project execution plan can be developed.

Stage 1 Preparation and Briefing

In this stage all the information should be compiled to allow the three-dimensional design to start on a stable basis including the brief and information about the site. In parallel the programme and process of design and construction can be fleshed out based on developing knowledge of the client's requirements.

The brief

The brief is the first design stage of a building, which is as important as any other piece of design, listing out the spaces and functions desired in the building. When the client tells the architect the spaces to go in the building, it can be useful to categorise the items as either 'requirements' or 'wants' so that the client and design team can have a basis on which to reduce the brief when the inevitable question comes about costs.

The brief includes a description and a floor area for each space. Sometimes this information is set out as a report with an area schedule, sometimes as a spreadsheet, and it can be cut up space by space into 'room data sheets'. The latter simply has all the data for each room on a separate sheet.

The space description may include many items of technical information such as:

The function of the space;
The expected number of occupants;
Space requirements;
Structural requirements;
Fire requirements;
Heat and cooling requirements;
Power and data;
Lighting;
Audio-visual and other services;
Acoustic criteria, both isolation from noise and internal reverberation;
Finishes;
Furniture and equipment.

Then it should talk about the use of the space and its desired relationship with other spaces.

The client's requirements do not just consist in the aforementioned technical items; they will also have more intangible desires to do with the look, atmosphere, image or philosophy of their new building. This information might be readily available, or it might be that it needs to be teased out of the client by discussion. A presentation of examples and ideas can be useful to prompt that discussion.

Feasibility study

The volume identified in the brief should fit on the site and be affordable within the client's budget, so a design exercise is often undertaken before the brief is written or in parallel with writing it to confirm these. This may be a feasibility study. The brief may then need adjusting in line with the conclusions of the feasibility study. Figure 9.3 shows a typical feasibility study plan.

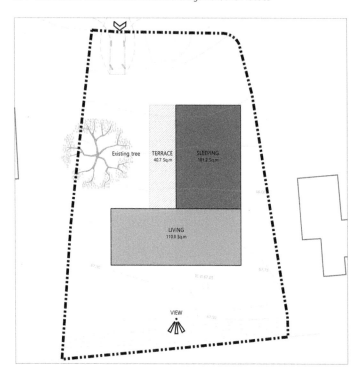

Figure 9.3 RIBA stage 1 Preparation and Briefing, feasibility study plan of a typical project

In the case of this project, a single-story house on a sloping site with a view, the criterion for establishing its feasibility is: can the desired area fit on the site? The plan is sufficient to show this can be done.

For other projects the criteria for feasibility might be different, for example: will the project be within the budget? In order to answer this question the project might need to be designed in some detail to establish a construction cost within an agreed percentage of certainty. Conversely there may be no need to carry out a feasibility study at all if the client has sufficient information to proceed with the project without one. Before embarking on a feasibility study the architect should establish with the client what question needs to be answered and therefore what work needs to be carried out to answer the question.

The purpose of an early design exercise like this can also be to sell the idea of the proposed building. There may be many people who need to be convinced that this building on this site is a good idea – the local community, potential tenants, investors, for example – and an early design accompanied by good images and other sales material can be part of this exercise. It may also help the client to organise their funds or internal approvals for the development. It is not uncommon for architects to be commissioned for a feasibility study, then to be stood down for a period before they are commissioned for the next phase of work. The project may even end completely if the design gets a bad reaction or is found to be unaffordable.

The feasibility study will help to align the brief with the project budget, however the study is inevitably lacking in detail so the budget can only be as accurate as the design at this stage. Experienced cost consultants will know how much the particular type of building will cost and they will put a contingency in the overall building cost to account for the approximate nature of the design information at the early stages. All this does not stop the design and budget becoming misaligned as the project progresses – either the design meets the brief but is over budget or the building is within the cost parameters but doesn't meet all the functional requirements. The design will need to be adjusted at every design stage to align it with the budget – this may involve a 'value engineering' exercise, see stage 3 Spatial Coordination, to bring down the cost of the design, or the budget may need to change to suit the design. The client will decide which of these is acceptable.

Site information
Information about the site should be collected either from existing drawings and other information or, if this is not sufficient, from a survey. For a smaller site, the architect

can visit and survey it themselves; for larger sites, surveyors can be commissioned. The surveys that may be needed include:

Topological: a survey of the geometry of the site and any existing buildings;

Utilities: a survey of the existing power, water drainage, telecoms and other services within and at the perimeter of the site;

Structural: a survey of the structure and its condition in any existing building;

Geotechnical: a survey of the ground conditions including trial pits or bore holes to establish the soil type, its bearing capacity and the level of the water table;

Arboricultural (trees);

Asbestos: this may be found in buildings constructed before 2000;

Archaeological: a 'desktop' survey of information about the history of the site may reveal enough information to establish whether a fuller archaeological survey of the site should be undertaken;

Flood risk assessment;

Environmental: if an environmental impact assessment will be required as part of the planning application, a survey should cover plants, birds and animals with particular attention paid to rare species such as voles, newts, bats, otters and the like.

In addition to information about the physical nature of the site, other information about its legal constraints is required:

Who owns it? The client may think he or she owns the site, but if there are any questions the ownership can be checked at the Land Registry.

Boundaries. What are the actual boundaries of the site? Are there any party walls?

Easements. These might be rights of way, rights to fish, rights to structural support, rights of light. There might be rights of adjoining owners, utility companies, the general public

or others to easements on your site, or the site might depend on easements from adjoining land.
Rights of light. Adjoining owners may have rights to light that will affect the allowable building envelope of the site.

For more information on the nature of easements, rights of light and other legal constraints on a site, see the *Architect's Legal Pocket Book* Chapter 4.

The planning guidance for the site will strongly influence what can be built on it. The local authority plan will show what use has been identified for the site, and the authority's guidance documents will indicate their policies for transport, green spaces, employment and many other topics. A review of recent planning applications for adjacent or similar sites within the local planning authority will yield valuable guidance about the types of developments that are likely to receive approval and whether there may be local opposition. Planning policy is described in Chapter 10 Planning.

Other bodies may either have a direct interest in a site or have the right to be consulted about new proposals for it – for example the Canal and River Trust, the Civil Aviation Authority, the Environment Agency and others.

Project execution plan (PEP)
At this stage the processes for the design, procurement and construction of the building should be set out in a project execution plan. This is a document that sets out how the project will be run, including the following headings:

Project description:

Project organisation: the design team, their roles, the responsibility matrix;
Programme;
Procedures for information exchange and communication: emails, letters, meetings, minutes, drawings;

Procedures for reviews;

Procedures for sign-off and for change control;

Information review and issue procedures for drawings and other information;

Site reviews and management of quality on site;

Programme and process for site tests;

The handover and completion processes;

Records to be handed to the client and those to be kept internally;

BIM strategy.

The project execution plan can be a standard office format that can then be tailored to suit the project, so it can grow to include more procedures for larger projects. For larger teams in particular the PEP ensures everyone will follow the same procedures and is informed about how the project is being run. Note that the PEP is part of the quality assurance structure of the practice and of the project, see Chapter 13 Quality assurance.

Stage 2 Concept Design

This is the stage at which three-dimensional design normally starts. The purpose of the stage is to establish all the main design ideas of the project. The primary elements to be completed as part of the concept design will vary depending on the building and the client's requirements, so the level of design resolution and the important elements where attention should be concentrated should be agreed with the client in advance. This agreement should be part of the project set-up at commencement.

The illustration in Figure 9.4 shows a typical plan for a house at RIBA 2 Concept Design stage. This will be accompanied by other drawings, by illustrations and by a stage design report.

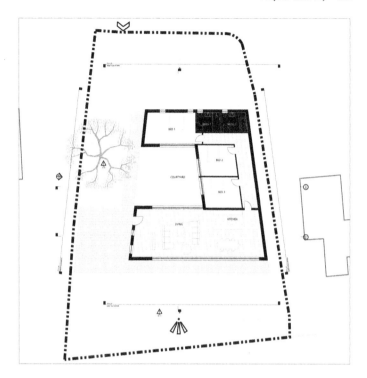

Figure 9.4 RIBA stage 2 Concept Design plan of a typical project

The concept design plan shows the design ideas for the project, a single-storey house on a sloping site.

The primary purpose of the concept design is to show an idea that can be agreed with the client. The level of development of the design at this stage should be agreed with the client and will vary depending on what is necessary to move the project forward. A cost will be important to confirm the acceptability of the design; a discussion might be required with the planning authorities or other interested parties; some structural or civil services engineering might be required; other studies might be required for planning or construction, and the deliverables should be produced to reflect these.

The level of design represented here meets the description of BIM LOD 100.

Client stage agreements

The client's agreement to the work done should be sought at the end of this and every stage before proceeding with any design work in the following stage. The nature of this sign-off should be agreed in advance: what information is required from the architect, engineers, cost consultant and so on; what presentations should be made; how long the client will need between receiving the information and giving the agreement; what exclusions or comments will be made and how these will be handled in the next design stage.

Stage 3 Spatial Coordination

This stage is important to complete the architectural design work, however the author has found that sometimes the purpose of such a stage needs to be explained to clients more than other stages.

Whereas the concept design represents the building in simple shapes, at the end of the spatial coordination phase all aspects of the design should be resolved:

Civil engineering;
Structural engineering;
Services design;
Interior design;
Lighting design;
Acoustic design;
Landscape;
Other technical specialisms.

Inevitably stage 3 overlaps to some degree with stage 4 Technical Design. Some products will need to be chosen at an early stage in the project if they are significant to the design, and others may need to be selected early if they need to be ordered a long time in advance of delivery.

The illustration in Figure 9.5 shows a typical plan for a house at RIBA 3 Spatial Coordination stage. The design has been

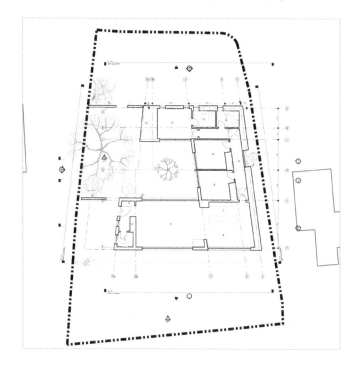

Figure 9.5 RIBA stage 3 Spatial Coordination stage plan of a typical project

The stage 3 diagram shows the developed design of a single-storey house on a sloping site.

The design has changed from the one shown at concept design where more detail has been added and the form of construction of all the parts of the building have been developed. All the engineering has been designed, materials and products have been chosen, the building is compliant with the regulations, so it is ready to be drawn for construction.

The final client's sign-off should be obtained at this stage before the building is tendered or issued to the contractor.

The level of design represented here meets the description of BIM LOD 300.

resolved so that all the structural engineering, services and other engineering elements are in their place, the method of construction of all the parts of the buildings are known and the elements are drawn at the correct sizes in the correct relationships to each other.

'Value engineering'
At some point in many projects the cost of the proposed design is above the identified budget, in which case a value engineering process should be carried out to bring the cost down whilst, so far as possible, retaining the essential functions.

Proposed cost savings should be fully studied before they are implemented to ensure they do not in fact result in cost increases. This can happen if, for example, the change lengthens the construction programme or requires additional scaffolding or temporary works. A saving might also not be beneficial if it compromises quality or performance or results in higher lifecycle costs.

The timing of value engineering
The cost of the building should be tracked regularly as the design progresses so that a cost overrun can be identified and dealt with as early as possible. It is easier to adjust the cost of the building design at the early stage of the design, and the ability to change the design reduces as work proceeds and decisions are made. Decisions may be difficult to change as they become embedded in the client organisation, and once the project is on site elements that have been built are difficult and expensive to change.

Conversely, if cost reductions are made too early in the project they may cut out parts of the building that it may be found later can be afforded.

The 'value engineering' process

Value engineering is best carried out in a positive, constructive and organised manner. With all the team working together the best outcome can be arrived at quickly. All aspects of the design should be considered to identify if every item that is going to be constructed is necessary: in the author's experience a 'shopping list' of potential cost reductions can be developed and analysed and then a number of them selected to achieve the required saving.

The aim of value engineering is to achieve the same end result more efficiently. The following questions can be asked:

- *What is the item or service?*
- *What does it do?*
- *What does it cost?*
- *What else would do the same job?*
- *What would that alternative cost?*

The essential quality, safety and performance requirements should be identified.

A five-stage process can assist a full analysis of the problem:

1   Information Phase
    What are the objectives of the value management process? What is the cost of the elements to be reviewed?
2   Creative and Speculation Phase
    A brainstorming workshop to talk through the alternatives can be useful, along with a request to all members of the team to bring their suggestions to the coordinator of the process.
3   Judgement and Analysis Phase
    Selection of the most useful suggestions to take forward. It can be helpful to select a range of potential savings, some simple to agree, some that will be more

difficult to implement and some that change the brief. By this process the team can analyse the client and stakeholders' appetites for fundamental questioning of the project.

4 Development and Investigation Phase
Investigate the chosen ideas to see what the design would be like incorporating the suggested change. Would there be an effect on the programme, on the construction method, on planning or other approvals? What would be the real cost saving accounting for any changes in programme, for the cost and time to redo any design work and allowing for elements to replace any elements removed?

To answer these questions the suggested saving item should be designed through to the current design stage by the architect and engineers and then costed and its impact analysed in terms of programme, construction, sustainability, statutory approvals, operational costs and effect on the functioning of the building, so that the implications of the change can be fully understood.

5 Recommendation and Selection Phase
The recommended changes can be presented to the client either completed or as a shopping list for the client to then decide. When the cost-saving change items to be implemented are agreed, they must be instructed and documented to ensure the changes to the design and, if required, the brief are recorded and understood.

Stage 4 Technical Design

In this phase the design is drawn to a greater level of detail and manufacturers' information is incorporated into the drawings and specification to bring the information to a level where it is ready to be issued to the contractor for construction. The specification will also be completed to describe all the elements of the design.

If the tender documents are issued at the end of stage 4 this will result in a contract price that is unlikely to change.

Even though the architect may finish his or her drawing work at this stage, if there are contractor design portions in the contract, or manufacturers are expected to input information, the design may change after stage 4 Technical Design. These changes may be handled either by the sub-contractor with the contractor design portion completing the drawing work of their element and other sub-contractors incorporating any design implications elsewhere in the building, or it may be handled by the architect continuing to update their drawings, or a mixture of both methods.

Drawings for construction

The illustration in Figure 9.6 shows a plan for a typical house at RIBA stage 4 Technical Design stage. All the parts of the building are fully resolved based on known products so that the design is ready for construction. References on the drawing are to other more detailed drawings and then to the specification. All the information required by the contractor to build the building is represented on a drawing or in the specification.

Specification

This is a written description of the building element by element.

The National Building Specification (NBS) [6] is a specification-writing online product that is easy to use, is based on British and European Standards and includes suggestions for products. It takes the user through the compilation of a specification based on the uniclass construction classification system.

If the architect is not confident of their knowledge to write a specification, or does not have the time, there are specialist

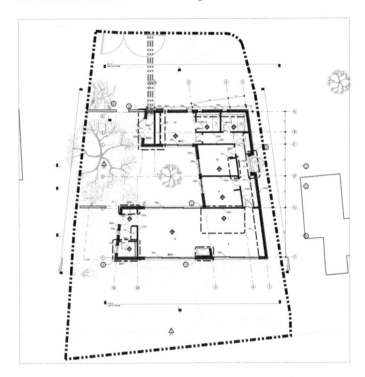

Figure 9.6 RIBA stage 4 Technical Design plan of a typical project

The stage 4 diagram shows the completed design of a single-storey house on a sloping site.

The design is the same as that illustrated in the stage 3 plan, now showing all the construction information. This includes dimensions, material and product references and structural, civil and services engineering design information as far as appropriate on an architectural drawing, all sufficient for the contractor to understand how to construct every element of the building. Not every item of the information is on this plan, so there are many references to other drawings or specifications which together as a set contain everything required.

The level of design represented here meets the description of BIM LOD 400.

companies who will take on this task, including such a service offered by the NBS.

The specification describes all the parts of the building either as systems, for example façade systems; as assemblies, for example doorsets; or as individual elements, for example ceramic tiles. The description can be written either as a performance specification in which the performance characteristic of the items are described for the contractor to fulfil, or as a prescriptive specification in which the item is described in complete detail. The specification should set out all the characteristics required of the item and refer to a manufacturer's product if desired. It should state what British, European or other standards the item is to meet. It should also describe how the item will be installed and the installation tolerances, site tests and quality control procedures. Most specifications will also have a section giving a general description of the project, including how the contractor is to respond to the specification, quality control, site conditions and the like.

Quality can be controlled on site by the use of samples of materials and construction. The author recommends three stages of construction quality samples:

(1) Samples of materials and elements. These to be submitted early in the process and signed off for appearance, fit with other elements and so on. The samples should be labelled and kept safe for reference and comparison with the installed items.
(2) Prototypes. Sample sections of parts of the building to show how elements fit together. This will give the design team and client an idea of how that part of the building will look and will give the contractor an opportunity to test the installation of various elements together.
(3) Benchmarks. The first item or area of any piece of construction, checked, amended to be right and approved before proceeding with that part of the work. This then becomes the quality standard for the remainder of the construction of the element or system.

These three should be described in the specification along with the process for approval of each.

Stage 5 Manufacturing and Construction

The architect's role may vary during the site phase. Under a traditional contract it may include administration of the contract, comment on contractors' drawings and site inspection. On larger projects the administration of the contract is likely to be carried out by a project manager, and in design-and-build contracts the architect's site inspection role may be reduced.

See also Chapter 12 Building contracts where the processes involved in managing a construction contract are described.

During this stage when the main contractor is responsible for getting the building built tensions can arise between the contractor's team and the design team. The tensions are most likely to arise over the subject of change. Change can come from many sources including:

Requests from the client or from bodies related to the client such as catering consultants and contractors, operators and facilities management organisations;
External parties such as utilities and adjoining owners;
Manufacturers and suppliers whose products, or the design of their installations, change aspects of the design;
Members of the design team who for one reason or another want or need to amend the design.

This is all assuming the design has been completed at the time of signature of the main contract. If the contract is a design-and-build, traditional contract with contractor's design portion, management contracting or a two-stage tender where some design work is continuing after tender, then there will be more change to accommodate.

The management of changes

All instructions should be confirmed in writing by the Contract Administrator. The client should not directly ask the contractors for a change verbally, as such matters should be in writing from the contract administrator. Since changes can cost additional money and can delay the construction, a process similar to the following should be established for them:

(a) An item – contractor's suggestion, product change, design idea, for example – is identified as something that will be a change and the client or project manager would like it to be investigated.

(b) A change control form, called 'Design Request' or similar, is initiated so the idea can be tracked. Figure 9.7 shows a typical Change Request format.

(c) The change proposal is then investigated to understand all its implications before it is instructed: the design team carries out an exercise to complete the design of the change in sufficient detail to understand all its implications; the contractor costs it and identifies the time it will take to carry it out.

(d) If the cost and time effects are acceptable, and the design is accepted, the change is instructed.

The programme, cost report and any other project documentation should be updated with the implications of the instructed change.

Review of contractors' drawings

Contractors will produce element or fabrication drawings, and the architect will be required to check them. Contractors will produce drawings under a design-and-build contract, sub-contractors will produce them if they have a contractor's design portion, and suppliers will produce them to develop the setting out and installation of their product into the building. In all cases these drawings constitute design work. The drawings

Change Request

Project	Project name		
Change request number	01	**Date**	day month year
Title	A brief description of the proposed change		
Requested by	Person proposing		

Description of the change
A fuller description of the change.

Attachments
Any drawings or other information describing the change.

Origin of the change
The reason for its suggestion

Work involved in
(a) Feasibility study
A description of the work involved for the architect and other members of the design and construction team to design the change to a level of detail for it to be costed and reviewed for a decision to be made.

(b) Implementation
A description of the work involved for the architect and other members of the design and construction team to design the change to a level of detail for it to be implemented.

Programme implication
The implications of the change on the design programme and the construction programme.

Design commentary
Any comments the architect, engineers or others may wish to add to give a better understanding of the change, its implications or why it is being proposed.

This Change Request has been issued as an item that may
    (i) have contract cost implications including programme implications,
    (ii) attract design team fees or
    (iii) affect the functionality of the building.

	Costs						
		Architect	**Structural engineer**	**Services engineer**	**QS**	**Contractor**	**Total**
(a)	Feasibility study						
(b)	Implementation						
	Total						

Date of instruction for (a) feasibility study			
To proceed		Not to proceed	
Date of instruction for (b) implementation			
To proceed		Not to proceed	

Figure 9.7 A typical Change Request form

should be checked thoroughly by the architect and engineers, though each only within the consultant's area of competence; thus comments should refer to the design and to the materials and products specified.

The convention is that the drawings should be returned to the contractor marked either:

'A' No comment.
'B' Comments. Incorporate comments and proceed with construction.
'C' Comments. Resubmit for review before construction.

The architect's review should be restricted to commenting only to ensure no instruction for change is given when reviewing a drawing. The comments should not develop the design or constitute a design change. If the drawings being reviewed affect other areas of the building, or their implication is a design change, that change should be fully designed by the architect and engineers to understand its implications and it should be instructed through the design change process.

Sub-contractors' development of their design can be a source of change affecting their own element and other adjoining elements.

Site inspections

Site inspection is one of the most important roles in the architect's scope of work. Architects regularly have claims made against them for failure to carry out this role correctly.

Defining the role

The starting point is to have the role clearly defined in the architect's appointment. There are three levels of inspection that are normally referred to:

(a) Commenting on general compliance with the design. The architect is not expected to check that all aspects of the design are being constructed correctly and in compliance with the drawings and regulations, only to see discrepancies from the design and regulations visible during infrequent visits. The frequency of site visits for this role is regularly identified as once a fortnight.

(b) Checking compliance with the drawings and regulations. The architect is expected to check that the building is being constructed in accordance with the design and regulations. To carry out this role the architect needs to visit site every other day or more frequently for small projects, and needs to be based on site for larger projects.

(c) Clerk of works. A clerk of works is based on site to check materials as they arrive and to check that construction as it is carried out is in accordance with the drawings and regulations. Clerks of works are often people with site experience who specialise in the role, moving from project to project. The architect may have a site inspection role in addition to the separate employment of a clerk of works.

It is important to know which type of inspection is included in the appointment, that it is clearly defined, that all parties understand what this means, and what is not included. The architect should ensure that they are visiting the site often enough to complete the inspection as described, and that their process of inspection will record and communicate what is inspected.

The site inspection role as defined in the Scope of Services section of the RIBA Standard Professional Services Contract 2020, for stage 5 Manufacturing and Construction, is:

> Carry out visual site inspections, as stated in item F of the Contract Details, to review the general progress of the works as they relate to the architectural design and issue site inspection reports to the Client.

This constitutes a review role as described in item (b) earlier so the architect needs to ensure they have sufficient fees for the time this role will take.

Site inspection records

All inspections on site should be recorded. When going on site the architect should take with them a set of drawings or specifications, notebook, camera and a tape measure. The purpose of a site inspection report is to record elements of the construction that are noticed to be not in accordance with the design information, and to record what has been built correctly. The site inspection report should be in writing and should contain:

- The date and time of the visit;
- A sequential number for the visit;
- The person carrying out the inspection;
- The item of work, clearly identifying the location including space within the building or site, location within the space, height above the floor or other measure so that people reading the report can find the unique item;
- Description of the item and the way in which it diverges from the design, referring to the drawing, specification clause and the like that it should comply with;
- Photograph of the item.

The inspection report should be issued to the contractor in writing on that day or within 24 hours of the visit.

Defective work

If work on site has been built not in accordance with the design information, the contractor is normally required by the building contract to rectify it at no cost to the client and with no delay to the programme.

If the architect wants to check an element of work that has been covered up, then he or she can request that it is uncovered to be inspected. If the uncovering or opening up involves time and workers, then there is a question as to whether the contractor or the client pays. Under clause 3.17 of JCT Standard Building Contract, SBC 2016, if the item of work is found to be defective then the contractor must bear the cost of opening up; if the work is constructed correctly then the client pays those costs.

Decisions about defective work can often be less clear cut than the architect might expect. The contractor may offer an alternative to the documented design in order to avoid the effort of redoing work, and this alternative will need to be analysed; perhaps it may constitute a change, which may need to be discussed and agreed with the client, and then instructed by the contract change procedure. Secondly the contractor may say that the work cannot be rectified as redoing it will delay the whole project, in which case some non-compliant work may have to be accepted, and again a judgement call will need to be discussed with the client, and the change may need to be analysed and instructed through the contract change procedure.

Stage 6 Handover

As the construction of a project approaches completion, a process is initiated to confirm the building has been constructed correctly and is acceptable to be occupied. In terms of construction the work needs to be checked to confirm it has been installed in accordance with the drawings and the design. In terms of its fitness to be occupied, all the safety systems must be demonstrated to be working correctly and any regulatory licences or sign-offs need to be obtained so that the building has the legal paperwork for occupation.

Construction sign-off
Certificate of Practical Completion
At the issue of a Certificate of Practical Completion, the building is handed back from the possession of the contractor to

the client. The issue of this certificate is the start of the defects liability period and has payment implications.

Before the certificate can be issued a process of checking and testing takes place, starting some weeks before the target date of completion to confirm the building is complete and in accordance with the design information.

The contractor presents the building as ready for inspection and the designers, architect, engineers and others walk round to record any items that are not complete or not constructed in accordance with the documentation. All such items, commonly called 'snags', should be clearly recorded with a description and photograph, if possible, and communicated to the contractor who will then rectify them. There are software programmes available to use on a mobile phone or tablet that will save time on the process of recording and communicating, see Chapter 14.

The list of defects should include:

- The date and time of the inspection;
- The person doing the inspection;
- A sequential number of the inspection;
- For each item: a unique identifying number for the defect;
- The location of the defect, including the space within the building or site, and the location within the space, including measurements to identify a unique location;
- The defect, including what is incorrectly constructed;
- Photographs.

The system, whether on paper or electronic, should include a method for recording that the item has been rectified and that the architect has then signed off that they have re-inspected it.

The building will also have to undergo a variety of tests to confirm that all the elements and systems in the building are functioning as required. Primarily these will be services-related tests, and additionally such items as waterproofing, doors and windows or other moving elements should be tested.

Regulatory sign-off

The building is required to comply with the Building Regulations and the local authority or private Building Control Approver will issue a Completion Certificate if requested to do so. The building may require other licences such as for food preparation, occupation if it is a public assembly building, storage of dangerous materials such as liquefied petroleum gas, and other functions.

The architect will be tasked with obtaining the Building Regulations certificate, and he or she should agree with the client or operator who will be responsible for obtaining the other licences.

Under the Building Safety Act Higher-Risk Buildings require a Completion Certificate from the Building Safety Regulator before they can be occupied.

Certain categories of building require a licence before they can be used: for example sports grounds that are hosting paying spectators will need a licence under the Sports Grounds Safety Act 1975, theatres and premises selling alcohol will require a licence under the Licensing Act 2003, premises selling food will need to be registered with the local authority, premises storing certain hazardous substances require a licence. Certain houses in multiple occupation, called 'HMOs', require a licence under the Housing Act 2004 and the Licensing of Houses in Multiple Occupation (Prescribed Description) (England) Order 2018. This is not a complete list of the premises and activities that require licences. The architect should check carefully what licences may be required if they affect the design of the building. The application for licences of this sort is normally likely to be the role of the client or occupier of the building.

Defects liability period

After the building is handed over to the client the contractor is responsible for defects arising from the construction process, not normal wear and tear, for a period, normally 12 months, though the default period in the JCT Standard Building Contract, SBC 2016, is six months. The architect may be involved in this period to check defects or discuss rectification. The defects are checked at the end of 12 months, and then the contractor is given an agreed period to rectify the items. When the defects are rectified the Final Certificate is issued ending the Defects Liability period, which is normally the end of the contractor's contract.

After a project is completed the project records need to be organised and filed in a method that they can be retrieved in future in case of a claim or if they need to be consulted for other reasons.

Records
RECORDS TO ISSUE TO THE CLIENT

The design and construction team is legally required to issue to the client a Health and Safety File and Fire Safety Information under the Building Safety Act.

The team should also issue a Building Manual, which may include the legally required information and incorporating technical information on all the parts of the building, to allow the client to maintain and replace items when they need to, and all other legal and practical information about the asset.

A Building User's Guide conveying in a simple format how the building works and how to use it.

The architect may compile the Building Manual, or it may be the contractor or a specialist consultant is better placed to complete this work.

RECORDS TO KEEP IN HOUSE
All project records should be kept, that is design information, including mark-ups of contractors' drawings, and management

information, including all records and correspondence, electronic or otherwise. This will need to be kept in case of legal challenges which could arise for some part of the life of the building. The standard period for legal liability under a contract is six years and under a contract signed as a deed is 12 years; however, under the Defective Premises Act 1972, claims can be made for up to 15 years so all project records must be kept for at least these periods.

End-of-project appraisal

The level of success of the project should be evaluated at the completion of the architects' work:

Design evaluation: what worked, what could be improved on? Did the design achieve the client's primary project aims, and did the building meet the brief?

Delivery processes: which were successful, how could they be improved?

Contractor's performance: in terms of quality of construction and management.

Design team evaluation: who amongst the design team worked well, how could the relationships be improved?

Financial evaluation: did the project make a profit?

Stage 7 Use

In the author's experience the architect is often not involved with their building after the handover processes are completed. This is a pity, and the RIBA has included 'Use' as a stage in the construction process to identify that learning from a completed building in use is vital to improvement for future projects.

A formal review can be organised with the client for them to give their view of how the building operates, where it works well and where it could be better. How was the process of design and construction, and what was the client's view of the good and bad points?

Some aspects of the building may not work as expected and may need to be adjusted after completion: this can be because people don't use the building as they were expected to do, or it could be that fashions or technology have changed since the design stage.

By feeding back knowledge to designers and to those commissioning buildings, the standards of design can be improved for further projects. A post-completion review can also deepen the relationship between the architect and the client, which can lead to further commissions.

Note

1 https://arb.org.uk/wp-content/uploads/2016/05/Architects-Code-2017.pdf

References

[1] RIBA Plan of Work. https://architecture.com/knowledge-and-resources/resources-landing-page/riba-plan-of-work
[2] Ostime, N. 2020. *RIBA Job Book*. London: RIBA Publishing.
[3] RIBA. 2020. *RIBA Standard Professional Services Contract 2020: Architectural Services*. London: RIBA Publishing.
[4] Speight, K. C. A. and Thorne, M. 2021. *Architect's Legal Handbook: The Law for Architects*. Abingdon and Oxfordshire: Routledge.
[5] Cousins, N. 2020. *Architect's Legal Pocket Book*. Abingdon and Oxfordshire: Routledge.
[6] The NBS (National Building Specification). https://www.thenbs.com

10
Planning

Introduction

Planning can be a complex area of architectural practice with many working parts and much riding on the success of a decision. Although architects carry out and administer a large number of applications, some seamlessly, it is a process that is fraught with complexities and so, if in doubt, it is recommended that appropriate advice be sought.

Planning is a responsibility that has been devolved to the administrations of England, Scotland, Wales and Northern Ireland.

Before a new building is built planning permission is required for the proposals (and for advertising, caravans, mineral workings and the storage and use of hazardous substances). There are some exceptions that allow certain types of buildings, extensions or alterations to be built without this permission, and in certain circumstances permission is also required before demolition of an existing building. If a building is constructed without planning permission the local authority can require it to be taken down, and breach of such an enforcement order is a criminal offence.

There is an enormous amount of law and policy guidance issued concerning planning, and land use more broadly, some of which may only be relevant for certain projects, for example laws governing public footpaths or access to open land. It should also be noted that planning laws and guidance on planning contained in the National Planning Policy Framework (NPPF) are updated regularly to reflect government policy. We cannot set out here all these laws and policy documents, so the references listed should be consulted to find out more.

DOI: 10.4324/9781003327288-13

Given the complexity of the regulations, when embarking on a new project the architect should carefully check the planning laws, the local policy documents and the map comprising the Local Plan (see later) as they relate to the specific site. The previous planning history of the site, if any, or of similar sites in the locality, will also give strong guidance as to what may be permitted. Furthermore, the services of a specialist planning consultant can be invaluable, particularly on larger and more complex projects.

Planning in England

The current system derives from the Town and Country Planning Act 1947, now superseded by the Town and Country Planning Act 1990, the Planning and Compulsory Purchase Act 2004, the Planning Act 2008 and supported by the NPPF introduced in 2012.

A key principle of planning under these acts is the concept of 'development' which covers building, engineering, mining and other operations and the making of any material change in the use of buildings or land, and although this may seem straightforward, is more complicated and has wide-reaching consequences.

The Local Plan

The planning authority for a locality may be a county council, district council, metropolitan district, a 'unitary authority' taking the function of district and county councils, or borough. In London the borough is the planning authority, though the Greater London Authority has the right to be consulted on some matters. The planning authority is required firstly to set out the planning policy, the Local Plan for their area, and secondly to administer the applications for permission. The Local Plan consists of a map plus a series of written policy documents setting out intentions for future development, assembled together into a Local Development Framework. There may also be Supplementary Planning Documents not part of the Local Plan but covering secondary topics relevant to planning applications.

When preparing a proposal for a site the Local Plan should be consulted early in the briefing process or even at stage 0, starting with the map, as the Local Plan will guide what can and cannot be built.

Permitted development

The General Permitted Development Order 1995 [1], last updated in 2022, lists over a hundred types of permitted development, all subject to many conditions, which may be summarised as:

- Works inside a dwelling house and some works to their exterior including extensions up to a certain size but importantly not a flats or maisonettes. See Permitted Development Rights for Householders, Technical Guidance, Ministry of Housing, Communities and Local Government, September 2019.
- Minor works.
- Changes of use within a Use Class (see Use Classes ahead).
- Temporary buildings and uses.
- Agricultural buildings.
- Certain industrial buildings.
- Mining operations.
- Demolition of an existing building, subject to confirmation by the local planning authority.
- Development by the Crown, certain government agencies and statutory undertakers.
- Development at amusement parks.
- Addition of a storey to existing residences in certain circumstances.

Note that these permitted development rights are restricted in Conservation Areas, National Parks, Areas of Outstanding Natural Beauty, World Heritage Sites and the Norfolk and Suffolk Broads, and do not apply to listed buildings.

The most significant permitted development right allows the conversion of existing offices and shops to housing, subject to Prior Approval and certain other restrictions.

Most permitted development categories are subject to conditions and one condition is that 'Prior Approval' must be sought from the local authority, or the authority must be asked if they will require an application for Prior Approval. Prior Approval allows the authority to consider certain aspects of the development such as transport and highways.

Local authorities may also restrict these rights by issuing an 'Article 4 Direction' which reinstates the requirement for planning permission to be sought.

Enterprise zones and similar

The Act contains powers enabling the government to identify different types of Simplified Planning Zones to encourage development and these may be used in Urban Development Areas and Enterprise Zones.

Permission required for demolition

Demolition is classed as 'development' under the Town and Country Planning Act 1990 and would therefore require planning permission, however it is then included as a class of permitted development under the General Permitted Development Order 1995. This inclusion will not therefore apply to listed buildings, those in National Parks, Areas of Outstanding Natural Beauty, World Heritage Sites and the Norfolk Broads.

Use classes

Use Classes for England are set out in the Planning (Use Classes) order 1987. A use class is a grouping together of similar land or building uses with some uses not even falling into these categories (which are called '*sui generis*', meaning in a class of its own). A change of use from one class to another normally requires planning permission, even if there is no building work involved in the change. The use classes are updated periodically and they can be seen on the Planning Portal [2].

The planning application process

The architect should decide the route through the planning process that is appropriate to the project and make sure they discuss and agree this with their client. Types of application:

Householder application;

Outline application. An application for permission for disposition of certain uses on a site, though not for the full design of the buildings;

Full planning application;

Listed building application;

Prior Approval. See permitted development;

Advertising consent application;

Lawful development certificate. A retrospective application to confirm a development was lawful;

Application for removal or variation of conditions;

Application for discharge of conditions;

Reserved matters;

Application for consent under a tree preservation order;

Application for a non-material amendment of an existing application.

The fundamentals of the process of application for planning approval are:

• Prepare proposals in accordance with the Local Plan.

If the proposals are not in accordance with the Local Plan they will have to be justified to the local authority and are less likely to be approved by the planning committee.

- Pre-application meeting.

  Meetings can be arranged with the officer in charge to discuss your proposals, with a view to getting their opinion in advance of submitting an application. The council will probably charge for the meeting. Pre-application meetings are very useful to ensure time and money are not wasted on an application that is unlikely to be approved, note however that the opinion of the officer will not be binding on the planning committee or authority.

  The authority will often request a submission of the proposal prior to a pre-application meeting and in some recent examples this submission has included information similar to a full application.

- Submit an application.

  This will include, as a minimum:

  - The local authority's application form, completed;
  - Ownership certificates and notices;
  - Notices under part 13 of The Town and Country Planning (Development Management Procedure) (England) Order 2015 stating that the applicant has contacted any existing owner, tenant or other person who has an interest in the site of the application;
  - Agricultural Land Declaration;
  - The appropriate fee (see the authority's website for their scale of charges);
  - Drawings fully describing the proposal to the appropriate level of detail. The information required will depend on the location and type of building, and the local authority's website should be consulted to understand what they are looking for;
  - Design and Access Statement. Required if a development is 'major', for one or more dwellings or relating to buildings of 100 m^2 or more or if the building is listed. The report should set out the design and describe its

features under all the topic headings relevant to planning (and for which many authorities still refer to the CABE guide 'Design and Access Statements: How to read, write and use them');

∘ If the development is likely to have significant environmental impacts the application must include an Environmental Impact Assessment (EIA) covering the topics set out in The Town and Country Planning (Environmental Impact Assessment) Regulations 2017 [3];

∘ Any other information requested by the local authority.

A 'Fire Safety Statement' may also be necessary for certain types of application (see following chapter regarding Building Regulations).

Planning applications are normally submitted online through Planning Portal [2] for all authorities in England and Wales and once 'validated' (i.e. when the authority confirms that it has sufficient information to commence the application process), the following formal processes may occur:

• Public consultation.
  For large or potentially controversial proposals the local authority will require the applicant to carry out public consultation including public exhibitions and meetings. These could include consultation early on in the design process to prepare a development brief. The larger the development and the greater its impact on the community the more consultation is likely to be requested.
• Publicity.
  The applicant must publicise a planning application so that neighbours are aware of it by site notices and by placing an advertisement in a local newspaper (see The Town and Country Planning (Development Management Procedure) (England) Order 2015, article 15) [4]. The local authority will also publicise the documents on its planning website.

Other than for Certificate of Lawfulness applications, the public has the right to make comment on the application within 14 days of the placing of the publicity notices and the local authority must take the representations into account.

- Local authority determination.

  A planning authority has eight weeks, or 13 weeks for a major development, or such other period as the authority and the applicant may jointly agree, to make a decision. A planning authority may make a decision via a planning committee but not exclusively, as some applications can be delegated to the planning officers themselves to determine.

  The authority has a duty to consult with the parish council of the development, with the county authority if relevant, with the Building Safety Regulator for relevant buildings, Historic England, the Environment Agency and a list of other government agencies. It may also consult with a range of other potentially interested bodies such as neighbourhood forums, water companies and others as appropriate.

- Conditions attached to a planning approval.

  A permission will normally be given with conditions which may be items to be complied with, such as times of working on site, or they may be items which require a further submission of information, such as requiring samples of the materials to be used.

  Conditions will be listed within a permission and precommencement conditions must be discharged before work can commence on site whilst others must be discharged before the occupation of the completed building, and these may require the submission of further information to the planning authority for approval before either of these two stages.

- The Community Infrastructure Levy (CIL) and Section 106 agreements.

  The CIL is an additional charge that can be levied on development to assist the authority with the construction of infrastructure. Authorities in England that have chosen to do so can charge a CIL on any new development creating new floorspace of 100 m^2 or more. Some developments may be eligible for exemption or relief from the levy subject to meeting certain criteria. The authority's website should give information about the levy rates and the procedures for applying for exemption or relief.

'Section 106 agreements' are obligations agreed between the local authority and the developer under section 106 of the Town and Country Planning Act 1990. They oblige the developer to pay for work outside the site that will enable the development, such as a new road junction, and are the subject of an agreement separate to the planning permission.

* Appeals

   If permission is refused or the applicant is unhappy with the conditions attached to a permission they can appeal to the Secretary of State within six months of the grant of permission. The Secretary of State appoints an inspector who will hear all the evidence and can also determine the appeal. The evidence can be written submissions, an informal hearing or a formal public inquiry depending on the complexity and public profile of the project. The Secretary of State also has the power to 'call in' applications made to local authorities to determine them him- or herself, normally in the case of large or controversial projects.

Planning permission lasts three years from the date of approval during which period development should commence, and a full planning application should be submitted within three years to grant of outline permission. Development is deemed to commence when a 'material operation', as defined by the act, has taken place on site such as demolition, construction of foundations or roads. There is a body of case law defining how much work on site is sufficient for development to be deemed to have commenced.

Non-material amendment

> This can be applied for if changes have been made to the scheme since planning approval. There is no definition of 'non-material amendment' and the local planning authority can decide what constitutes such an amendment.

Lawful development certificate

An owner can apply for a Lawful Development Certificate (called a 'Certificate of Lawfulness' in the act) to confirm that an existing or proposed use or development is lawful. This might be useful to either establish that an existing use has been established following the passage of time even if a planning application wasn't originally sought or if works are proposed that are expected to come under the permitted development rules, but either there is some doubt, or the sale of the property requires confirmation of the building's status. They can also be useful to confirm if the failure to comply with a planning condition is lawful or any other matter. An application for a Lawful Development Certificate is made to the local authority, it must contain sufficient information for them to be able to make a decision and it will attract a fee.

Planning in Scotland

In Scotland the main statute is the Town and Country Planning (Scotland) Act 1997 and the Planning (Scotland) Act 2019 [5], supported by the National Policy Framework.

The planning system is largely similar to that in the rest of the United Kingdom with a National Planning Framework, Regional Spatial Strategies and Local Development Plans setting out the structure for development. The use classes are different from England and Wales, as are the detail of the classes of permitted development. The latest legislation in Scotland on this topic is The Town and Country Planning (General

Permitted Development and Use Classes) (Scotland) Miscellaneous Amendment Order 2023 [6] which sets out the latest use classes and permitted development categories.

Section 75 agreements mirror section 106 agreements in England and Wales, but there is no Community Infrastructure Levy in Scotland.

The application process is similar to England and Wales and can be made online through the planning Scotland website [7]. Permission is required for demolition.

Planning in Wales

Planning law in Wales is largely based on the same Acts as in England. The Planning (Wales) Act 2015 strengthens the 'plan-led' approach to planning in Wales, with the development of a National Development Framework, and Strategic Development Plans for issues which are relevant across local authority boundaries. The Act requires or permits certain planning applications to be made directly to the Welsh Ministers rather than to local planning authorities and introduces a statutory pre-application procedure for certain categories of planning application. The Act also makes changes to development management and enforcement and increases the transparency of the appeal system.

Applications can be made online through the Welsh Government website [8].

Planning in Northern Ireland

In Northern Ireland the primary planning legislation is the Planning Act (Northern Ireland) 2011.

The system in Northern Ireland is similar to that in the rest of the UK with the Department for Infrastructure responsible for regional policies and the 11 local councils responsible for their

Local Plans and the determination of most applications. If an applicant is unhappy with a planning decision they can issue an appeal which will be heard by the Planning Appeals Commission, a body that is independent of the department. The application for appeal must be made within four months of the decision.

Applications can be made online through the Northern Irish Government website [9].

Historic buildings

The National Heritage List for England, or 'The List', originated in 1882, when the first powers of protection were established. These developed into what we know today as statutory 'Listing' just after the Second World War (and which differs to a building being 'locally listed' by a planning authority).

Buildings and other items of historic interest can be protected by being included in the list of buildings of historic and architectural interest or by inclusion in a conservation area [10]. The list is administered in England by the Historic Buildings and Monuments Commission for England, called 'Historic England' [11], the Royal Commission for the Ancient and Historical Buildings of Wales [12] in Wales and Historic Environment Scotland [13] in Scotland.

There are three grades of listing:

Grade 2: buildings of special interest;
Grade 2*: particularly important buildings of more than special
    interest;
Grade 1: buildings of exceptional interest.

Generally grade 2 relates to the exterior of the building and grade 1 preserves the interior and exterior, however the entry in the list will describe the specific elements of the building that are of historic or architectural importance. Note that monuments, parks and gardens, battlefields and wrecks at sea can also be protected.

Any work to a listed building, including demolition, requires listed building consent, which is an additional application to normal planning application. The listed building consent lasts three years. There are various mechanisms under the Act to enforce it, including criminal status sanctions, to prevent owners allowing listed buildings to deteriorate and to prevent buildings being demolished whilst their potential addition to the list is being considered.

Listed building heritage partnership agreement

To agree and carry out works to a listed building, a Listed Building Heritage Partnership Agreement [14] can be set up between the local authority and one or more private individuals or organisations involved with the building. The purpose of such an agreement is to set out works to be done in the framework of a vision for the future and use of the building, and in return agree listed building consent, without having to make supplemental applications for minor items.

Conservation areas

Conservation areas are administered by local authorities who will seek to preserve the character of the locality when considering planning applications and where a key test is whether the application's proposals will 'preserve and enhance' this. The protection given to buildings within a conservation area is similar to that for listed buildings. An application is required for demolition within a conservation area.

References

[1] The Town and Country Planning (General Permitted Development) (England) Order 2015.
[2] The Website for Planning Applications in England. www.planningportal.co.uk

[3] The Town and Country Planning (Environmental Impact Assessment) Regulations 2017.

[4] The Town and Country Planning (Development Management Procedure) (England) Order 2015.

[5] The Planning (Scotland) Act 2019.

[6] The Town and Country Planning (General Permitted Development and Use Classes) (Scotland) Miscellaneous Amendment Order 2023.

[7] Scottish Government Planning Application. https://www.eplanning.scot

[8] Welsh Government Planning Application. https://www.gov.wales/apply-planning-permission

[9] Northern Irish Government Planning Application. https://www.nidirect.gov.uk/articles/making-planning-application.

[10] The Planning (Listed Buildings and Conservation Areas) Act 1990.

[11] The List. https://historicengland.org.uk/

[12] Listed Buildings in Wales. https://cadw.gov.wales/advice-support/cof-cymru/search-cadw-records

[13] Listed Buildings in Scotland. https://www.historicenvironment.scot/advice-and-support/listing-scheduling-and-designations/listed-buildings/search-for-a-listed-building/

[14] Setting up a Listed Building Heritage Partnership Agreement, Historic England Advice Note 5, Historic England, November 2015.

11
Building control and CDM

Introduction

Building control – the writing of the Building Regulations and the process of approval and enforcement of their implementation – is a responsibility that has been devolved to the administrations of England, Scotland, Wales and Northern Ireland.

The purpose of the Building Regulations is to control the standards of construction to ensure that buildings are safe for their occupants from fire, structural collapse, slips, trips and falls; that their water supply, ventilation and drainage will ensure a healthy environment; that they will use the minimum of energy; and that in other ways create an acceptable environment. As such, they are distinct and separate from planning regulations, see Chapter 10 Planning, that tend to deal with a building's use and appearance as part of land use planning but can be more technical in nature, and can get confused with Building Regulations and be considered the same particularly by some domestic clients.

The Building Regulations

Any new building in the United Kingdom must comply with the Building Regulations, and contravention of procedural or technical requirements is an offence for which a local authority can take enforcement action.

The primary legislation empowering these aspects of the control of construction come from the Building Act 1984 which has been amended by many succeeding acts. The Building

DOI: 10.4324/9781003327288-14

Regulations themselves, schedule 1 of the regulations, are short, and it is them with which buildings need to comply. The relevant section of schedule 1 is set out at the beginning of each of the Approved Documents.

The Approved Documents give practical guidance on how to meet the requirements of the Building Regulations in common construction situations. They do not cover every form of construction, particularly not innovative or unusual methods. Following guidance of the Approved Documents will tend to lead to compliance with the Regulations, but will not guarantee it. The designer is strongly advised to follow the Approved Documents, but they can achieve compliance with the Regulations by using alternative methods of compliance (such as those set out in British Standards – see later) that will need to be justified to the approving body. However, a key aspect of this is that a designer can't 'mix and match' parts of an Approved Document with other guidance and should only use one method or the other, not a blend.

The Approved Documents for England are:

A Structure;
B Fire safety;
C Site preparation and resistance to contaminants and moisture;
D Toxic substances;
E Resistance to sound;
F Ventilation;
G Sanitation, hot water safety and water efficiency;
H Drainage and waste disposal;
J Combustion appliances and fuel storage systems;
K Protection for falling, collision and impact;
L Conservation of fuel and power;
M Access to and use of buildings;
O Overheating;
P Electrical safety;
Q Security in dwellings;

R   Infrastructure for electrical communications;
S   Infrastructure for charging electric vehicles;
T   Toilet accommodation;
7   Materials and workmanship.

This book will not set out the detail of the regulations and Approved Documents themselves which can be looked up on:

England: https://www.gov.uk/topic/planning-development/
      building-regulations
Wales: https://gov.wales/building-regulations-guidance
Scotland: https://www.gov.scot/policies/building-standards/
      monitoring-improving-building-regulations/
Northern Ireland: www.buildingcontrol-ni.com/regulations

Note that the regulations are updated frequently so the reader should ensure they are referring to the latest versions.

The Approved Documents form the core of the documentation to achieve compliance, and there are other important documents that should be referred to in certain circumstances:

BS9991: 2015, Fire safety in the design, management and use
      of residential buildings – code of practice.
Gives additional guidance on the fire safety design of residen-
      tial buildings.
BS9999: 2017, Fire safety in the design, management and use
      of buildings – code of practice. Gives additional guidance
      on the fire safety design of buildings. This guides the de-
      signer to a risk-assessment approach to fire safety for more
      complex buildings or where the Approved Documents are
      not being followed.

The Regulatory Reform (Fire Safety) Order 2005 sets out a method for building owners or managers to assess and man-age the fire safety of their premises once completed through risk assessments. A 'Responsible Person' is identified to carry out the risk assessments and to implement any changes to the building, its management or use that may be identified from the assessments. The local fire authority carries out some checking of premises to ensure the process is being followed and that the buildings are safe.

It should be noted that some building types have a regulatory regime additional to the Building Regulations, for example sports grounds requiring a safety certificate where the Guide to Safety at Sports Grounds written by the Sports Grounds Safety Authority is the guiding document for the spaces and functions specifically related to sport. Health buildings and education buildings are similarly covered by additional regulations. Some of these additional documents are:

The Guide to Safety at Sports Grounds, 6th edition, the Sports Ground Safety Authority, 2012. A guide giving recommendations for all aspects of design of sports grounds that will require a safety certificate.

Health Building Notes and Health Technical Memoranda. There are a series of these [1] published by the National Health Service that give guidance on all aspects of the design of buildings for the NHS.

Educational buildings. The government publishes a series of Area Guidelines and Net Capacity, Employer's Requirements, Strategic Design Advice, Baseline Designs [2] and Building Bulletins [3] for nurseries and schools.

Some buildings controlled by other legislation are exempt from the Building Regulations:

Buildings controlled by the Manufacture and Storage of Explosives Regulations 2005, the Nuclear Installations Act 1965 except for dwellings offices, canteens and the like on nuclear sites, a scheduled monument under the Ancient Monuments and Archaeological Areas Act 1979.

Exemptions from the Building Regulations

The regulations list seven categories of construction work that do not require Building Regulations approval:

(1) Work controlled by other legislation, see earlier;
(2) Buildings not frequented by people, for example plant rooms that would be visited infrequently, with exceptions;
(3) Greenhouses;
(4) Temporary buildings, defined as a building that is not intended to be in place for longer than 28 days;
(5) Ancillary buildings, defined as site accommodation;
(6) Small detached buildings, defined as no more than 30 m^2 provided they have no sleeping accommodation and are not within 1 m of any site boundary, or otherwise 15 m^2;
(7) Certain small extensions.

Note however these works may require planning approval.

There were also some local acts around the country related to buildings, notably the London Building Acts, which have generally been superseded by the national building regulations. Part 30 of the London Building Acts dealing with temporary buildings remains in force for the inner London area.

The regulations also refer onwards to many British Standards (BS) European Norms (EN) and other documents that give guidance on more detailed aspects of construction materials, assembly and systems, designing and other matters.

The process of building control

Anyone carrying out building work or a material alteration must issue a building notice or submit a full plans application (called 'Building Control Approval with Full Plans') to the local authority who has a duty to enforce the regulations. 'Building work' is defined in regulation 3 as the erection or extension of a building, a material change of use or material alteration. A 'material alteration' is defined as one which would result in the building not meeting the requirements of the regulations where previously it had, or being more unsatisfactory than before. There are a few exemptions where building work does not need to comply as described previously.

In terms of timing, it is accepted that a building should comply with the regulations in force at the time the Building Regulations application was issued and does not have to take account of changes published after that date. This accepted rule is subject to transitional arrangements for the regime under the Building Safety Act and also subject to a requirement to commence work.

The owner or developer of a building must obtain approval from a certifier that the building complies with the Regulations, either the local authority or a private approved inspector. Under the Building Safety Act approved inspectors, whether private or in local authorities, are called Building Control Approvers and are registered by the Building Safety Regulator. It should be noted however that their certification does not replace the owner or developer's legal requirement to comply with the Regulations. Work to HRBs under the Building Safety Act is the subject of a different checking and approval regime, see later.

Dispensations and relaxations

The Secretary of State, or the certifying body, has the power to dispense with or relax elements of the Building Regulations if they consider the application of the regulations would be unreasonable in the circumstances. It is the author's advice that dispensations or relaxations of the regulations, however small, should be treated with caution by architects and builders as their legal basis will be questionable even if backed up by a formal agreement in writing from the approving authority in accordance with the Acts. The burden still sits with the building owner, and their designers and contractors, to ensure compliance with Regulations.

The Building Regulations application and approval process in England and Wales

A Building Regulations application can be issued to either the local authority or a private Building Control Approver. Note that only local authorities can take enforcement action, so a private approver may hand a project back to the local authority if there is a problem that requires enforcement action. When they start work on a project private approvers must give an initial notice to the local authority advising that they are taking over the building control function. The date at which the application is deemed to have been made is then the date of this notice.

The design team may find it helpful also to employ a building regulations consultant to advise on the design to achieve compliance with the regulations.

Building notice

A notice is deposited with the local authority and work can start on site provided the authority is given two days' notice. The authority can request further information and should then visit the works as they progress to inspect, during which they can issue directions for the works to be altered if they consider they fall short of the standard expected. The Building Notice procedure is generally used for smaller items of work and cannot be used for offices, shops or other major buildings.

Building control approval with full plans

Information is submitted to the authority with the appropriate fee or to the private approver. The information should consist of sufficient drawings, specifications, calculations and reports to demonstrate compliance with the regulations.

The authority may pass or reject the plans within five weeks, or eight weeks by mutual agreement, and once the plans have been deposited work can start on site provided the authority is given two days' notice.

Most often authorities will give an approval subject to conditions, and if further information is needed to demonstrate compliance this will be included in the conditions.

Although this process clearly takes longer than the aforementioned building notice procedure, a key advantage is that should the authority approve the plans submitted, if the development is carried out in accordance with these plans, then even if the authority visits a site to inspect and request a change, this need not necessarily be followed.

The approver may want to visit the site to see foundations, in-ground drainage and other works before they are covered up, and they should be given notice in advance to allow them to do so. They may also want to test elements to confirm their compliance. The authority will define the inspections it will undertake before work starts and communicate this to the applicant.

The Building Safety Act 2022

The Building Safety Act 2022 [4] created a new body, the Building Safety Regulator (BSR) for England and Wales, to oversee the safety and performance of all buildings and also to act as the approving body for Building Regulations applications for Higher Risk Buildings (HRB), primarily high-rise (i.e. over 18 metres or seven storeys) housing but also hospitals and care homes.

It is important to understand that although additional processes are now required for HRBs, there are also requirements under the Building Safety Act that are applicable to all building projects. Although contravention of the Building Regulations has always been a criminal offence, the Act includes changes to the timescales of enforcement, an increase in the availability of enforcement tools and an increase in the severity of punishments for contravention.

Under the Act and in relation to HRBs there are three 'gateways' of regulatory approval which a project must get through – the first as part of a planning application, the second the Building Regulations application and the third the sign-off of the completed building for occupation.

Accompanying these is what is called the 'golden thread' of safety information applicable to HRBs. The intention of the 'golden thread' is that clear information about the safety design of the building should follow through from planning to completion so that the owners and users can see how the building is intended to work, how they should use it and what they need to do to maintain the safety systems.

The Building Regulations process for HRBs is more exacting than for other types of buildings. An application for approval for an HRB will go to the Building Safety Regulator, not a local authority or private inspector, who will not allow construction to start until the drawings are approved.

An application must also be made for changes in the design that have occurred after the first set of information has been issued and again construction cannot proceed until the change is approved. The applicant is required to make a separate application for a completion certificate and the building cannot be occupied until they have received the certificate.

The BSR assembles a team of architects and engineers for each application. As part of building control this multi-disciplinary team (MDT) is involved throughout the construction process. It sets an inspection schedule and provides a lead contact for applicants.

The dutyholders for construction under the CDM regulations – client, designers, principal designer, contractor and principal contractor – have new duties under the Building Safety Act. Dutyholders need to work together to plan, manage and monitor the design work and the building work, ensure they cooperate and communicate with each other, coordinate their work and have systems in place to ensure that building work, including design work, complies with all relevant Building Regulations.

The regulations also set out the competence requirements, defined as 'the skills, knowledge, experience and behaviours' that those dutyholders will need to have to undertake their work and to ensure that those they appoint are in turn competent to carry out their work.

There is an ongoing control process for the management of fire and structural safety risks for HRBs through their life as occupied buildings. All HRBs should be registered with the BSR and an 'accountable person' identified who will be responsible to the BSR for the management.

At the time of writing the processes under the Building Safety Act are new so there is little experience of their use.

The building standards application and approval process in Scotland

Before starting work on a construction site in Scotland a Building Warrant must be obtained for most types of building. An application is made to the local authority Building Standards department, or a private Approved Certifier of Design or Construction can certify to the local authority that the design complies with Building Standards. The application should include drawings and other design information, a form and a fee. Starting construction without a warrant is an offence.

The Scottish Building Regulations are supported by Technical Handbooks for domestic and non-domestic buildings, equivalent to the English Approved Documents.

The Building Regulations application and approval process in Northern Ireland

The process in Northern Ireland is similar to that in England and Wales – a full plans application can be made to request approval of drawings and other information in advance of starting on site, or a building notice can be submitted for smaller works.

The Regulations are supported by a series of Technical Booklets equivalent to the English Approved Documents.

Construction health and safety (CDM)

The motivation for the improved regulation of health and safety on building sites was the unacceptable number of injuries and fatalities occurring in the construction industry. In 1990 and 1991 the EU Council of Ministers agreed to issue directives on this matter and the UK regulations are the result of this Europe-wide initiative. Although sometimes criticised in the industry for the amount of paperwork generated, there has been a reduction in the number of deaths and injuries on construction sites since its introduction.

The current regulations are the Construction (Design and Management) Regulations 2015. They create duties for the client, designer and contractor. The management of the duties under the regulations is given primarily to a 'Principal Designer' and 'Principal Contractor'.

The client must appoint in writing a Principal Designer and a Principal Contractor for any project of sufficient size and ensure that the processes are being followed. The client must ensure the Health and Safety Executive (HSE) is notified before the construction phase begins. The HSE must be notified where the construction work is likely to last longer than 30 working days and have more than 20 workers working simultaneously at any point, or exceed 500 person days. It is one of the architect's duties to ensure the client is aware of their role and responsibilities under the regulations.

The Principal Designer, who should normally be the architect, co-ordinates the CDM process during the design stage. Whether appointed as the Principal Designer or not, the architect has a duty to design the building to reduce the safety risks to construction workers, maintenance staff and those using the building as a place of work. The Principal Designer should pass their information about the design on to the contractor. A Health and Safety File should be produced at the end of the project containing information about the project emphasising the safety aspects of the building, either by the Principal Designer or by the Principal Contractor if the duty has been passed to them.

The Principal Contractor shall, before they start on site, prepare a Construction Phase Plan setting out how they intend to carry out the construction works in a safe way. This should be reviewed and updated as the works proceed.

At completion the Health and Safety File is passed to the client.

References

[1] Health Building Notes. https://www.england.nhs.uk/estates/health-building-notes/
[2] https://www.gov.uk/government/collections/school-design-and-construction/
[3] https://www.gov.uk/government/publications/primary-and-secondary-school-design/
[4] The Building Safety Act 2022. https://www.legislation.gov.uk/ukpga/2022/30/section/33/enacted

12
Building contracts

Introduction

Building contracts – the contracts between clients and builders for the construction of buildings – fall into three broad categories: 'traditional', 'design-and-build' and 'management'. Within each category there are variations and the boundaries between the categories can be blurred.

This chapter sets out the main forms of contract used in the United Kingdom and discusses the primary clauses used in the management of a typical contract.

The diagrams in Figures 12.1 to 12.4 show the relationships between the main parties in the various forms of building

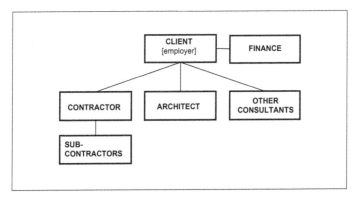

Figure 12.1 A diagram showing the contractual relationships in traditional contracting. The lines represent contractual relationships

DOI: 10.4324/9781003327288-15

contracts. Numbers of other parties are represented by the boxes labelled 'sub-contractors' and 'other consultants'. The lines between the boxes represent contracts between the parties. Note that the architect and other consultants have a role to play in the contract between the client and main contractor, which is discussed next.

Traditional contracts

The 'traditional' form of contract is suitable for any size of project and is commonly used for small to medium-sized projects, particularly domestic projects. The client employs the architect and other consultants to 'design' the building, then employs a contractor to then build it. In the author's opinion the traditional form should be used in preference to any other form wherever possible.

In its simplest form the architect and other design consultants are fully responsible for all design work and the contractor only builds. In practice there is usually some element of design work by the contractor, whether specialist elements like stairs or windows in a domestic project or curtain walling, piling or other elements of a larger, more complex one.

The contract tender should be issued when all the design work is completed to achieve an accurate price and to ensure there are no changes during the contract.

Advantages:

- Clear responsibilities for design and construction.
- Allows the client fully to control the project, particularly design and specification.
- Certainty of cost and programme is achieved if the design is completed before tender.

Disadvantages:

- The overall project programme can be longer as the tender is issued after completion of all the design.
- There is more work for the client than in other forms as they must manage the contractor and consultants.
- The standard contract allows mechanisms by which the contract sum and programme can increase if there are valid reasons for these to change ('relevant events').

Design-and-build contracts

A design-and-build contract is one where the client employs a contractor who then employs an architect, other design consultants and sub-contractors. Before the design-and-build contract can be procured a set of 'employer's requirements' (ERs), which may include a design, has to be prepared to form the basis of a tender. For this the client initially employs a design team who develop a scheme sufficient to issue for tender. When the contractor is then appointed, 'contractor's proposals' (CPs) are created that the employer is asked to accept and the design team may be 'novated' or 'switched' across to the contractor's employment where they complete the CP scheme including all the associated design work.

When a client appoints a design-and-build contractor they often also employ a team of consultants – identified in Figure 12.2 by the box labelled 'advisors' – to ensure the project is being designed and built to meet their requirements. This might be architects, engineers, quantity surveyors and others.

There are two main reasons why this form of contract might be chosen over a traditional form: firstly, the tender can be issued earlier in the design process. This can have the perceived effect of reducing the overall programme for the project, something of great interest to many clients who want a building

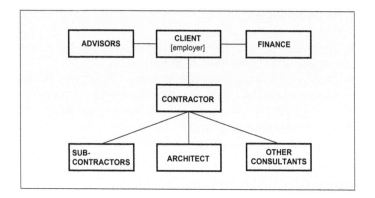

Figure 12.2 A diagram showing the contractual relationships in a design-and-build contract. The lines represent contractual relationships

completed quickly, for commercial or other reasons. Secondly, unless a client changes their requirements, they should have a fixed price and programme for the delivery of their 'order', i.e. building. Lastly, this arrangement involves the client in less management than a traditional contract as they only have a single contract and single relationship to the main contractor, who then manages all the other parties as a 'one-stop shop'. Some clients do not have the ability or the inclination to manage a construction project and would rather hand the responsibility to a contractor.

However, within this basic idea of 'design-and-build' there is a great deal of variation in practice. One element is the completeness of the employer's requirements or design at the moment of issue for tender. It can be quite preliminary – RIBA stage 2 Concept Design or even stage 0 Strategic Definition. This brings the contractor on board earlier in the project and leaves them more room to develop their CP design. Conversely the ERs could be a fully-fledged design that can be issued when it has reached the end of stage 4 Technical Design. This arrangement leaves very little for the contractor to design, and the primary purpose of a tender this late in the project is purely to transfer liability from the employer to the contractor.

Advantages:

- The overall project programme can be shortened as the design can be completed whilst the contractor is starting on site.
- The client only has one point of contact for the project so has less management work than with a traditional contract and a single point of liability.
- The client has a single cost and programme for the project that includes all professionals.
- The client can negotiate a lump sum that takes away the risk of cost increases.

Disadvantages:

- The client loses control of the design by handing design responsibility to the contractor with their ERs. This can lead to a reduction in the quality of the end product.
- If the client requests design changes they may be more expensive or have greater programme implications than under a traditional contract.

Design-build-and-finance, design-build-finance-and-operate

The role of the contractor can also extend further than just contracting into financing, maintaining and even managing the completed building. A typical example of this type of arrangement would be a government agency that wants to acquire a building but does not want to finance or run it, so they issue a tender for a company or consortium to finance, design, construct and operate the facility, with the government agency possibly providing the land and ownership reverting to them after 30 years. The company or consortium then has 30 years in which to make a profit on the project. The contract form in this example would probably be an individual bespoke arrangement.

Some government projects have been constructed under a form of design-build-and-finance called 'private finance initiative' of 'PFI' for short.

Management contracts

Management contracts come in two forms: firstly, where a construction manager and all the sub-contractors are employed by the client directly, called 'construction management', and secondly where the client employs a contractor who employs the sub-contractors and manages them, but does no construction itself, called 'management contracting'. Both forms can involve more or less design work by the sub-contractors.

Construction management

In construction management the client holds all the contracts with the designers, the construction manager and the sub-contractors. The management contractor is appointed first, then

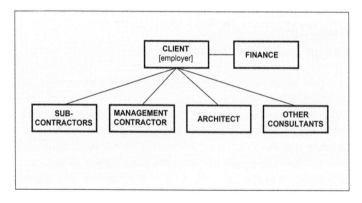

Figure 12.3 A diagram showing the contractual relationships in a typical construction management arrangement. The lines represent contractual relationships

the sub-contracts are tendered so that an overall price is only known when the last sub-contractor is appointed. This gives the ability for the overall project cost to be controlled if it is managed in the right way.

The architect and other design consultants can carry out all the design work or the sub-contractors can have some design responsibility.

Advantages

- By appointing a construction manager early in the project advice can be gained about management of the construction process.
- Construction work can start before all the sub-contracts have been tendered, thus shortening the overall project programme.
- Costs can be managed closely to get a lower overall cost.

Disadvantages

- This type of contract involves more management work for the client.
- There is no fixed price until the last sub-contractor is appointed.

Management contracting

In management contracting the client holds a single contract with the management contractor who holds the contracts with the sub-contractors but themselves perform a purely management function. The contractor can be appointed early on in the design work to give advice on construction methods, timing and the like. They then tender the sub-contracts and again the overall project cost is only known when the last sub-contractor is appointed.

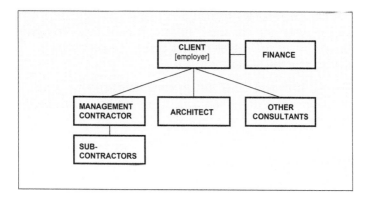

Figure 12.4 A diagram showing the contractual relationships in a management contracting arrangement. The lines represent contractual relationships

The architect and other design consultants can carry out all the design work or the sub-contractors can have some design responsibility.

Advantages

- By appointing a management contractor early in the project advice can be gained about management of the construction process.
- Construction work can start before all the sub-contracts have been tendered, thus shortening the overall project programme.
- Costs can be managed closely to get a lower overall cost.

Disadvantages

- There is no fixed price until the last sub-contractor is appointed.

Which contract type?

The architect may be asked to advise their client on the most suitable contract arrangement for their project so should understand the main types of procurement, their advantages and disadvantages, their opportunities and risks. They should understand tendering processes, how the different contract types affect the management of construction, and their effects on the project outcomes. If the architect is unsure on these subjects they should seek specialist advice.

In Chapter 2 on the construction industry we talked about the Latham and Egan reports that recommended a more collaborative approach between the parties in construction projects. They also promoted more off-site manufacturing and technological improvements. These matters should form part of the discussions about construction processes.

There are three primary factors to take into account when choosing the type of procurement arrangement, which are often in tension and must be kept in balance – cost, quality and time:

If a building is cheaper the quality is likely to be lower.
If the quality of a building is higher it is likely to be more expensive and take longer to build.
If a building is to be built quickly it might be more expensive and have lower quality.

Additional to these three are other matters to take into account that may be important to the client and the project which are discussed ahead. Figure 12.1 also lists out some of the issues related to cost, quality and time to be taken into account in the choice of contract type:

• The size and complexity of the project.
  A smaller project, such as a house for example, can be managed under a simpler, probably traditional, contract

form. For a larger project with more complex design and construction and a larger team of consultants, design-and-build or a management form of contract may be make the delivery of the project easier for the client.

- The client's ability and inclination to be involved in managing the project.
  More sophisticated clients who regularly manage construction projects, such as government agencies or developers, will be more willing to take on management activities and associated risk in order to obtain a better price and a better product. Clients who are building one building or do not have the time to spare from their normal business may want a consultant or contractor to manage their project for them.
- The client's desire to control the works.
  If the client is very interested in the detail of the finished building they are better placed if they are employing the architect and other designers directly throughout the course of the project, for example if the quality of finishes is important for their business or they are working on a historic building. This can be in a traditional contract or a management form.
- The allocation of risk.
  If a client does not want to take on board responsibility for cost or programme overruns they can pass this on to the contractor, probably through a design-and-build arrangement.

It is the author's view that the traditional form of contract should be used wherever possible. In recent years questions have been asked about design-and-build contracts, particularly about whether the design function is always carried out by people with the qualifications and experience to make the correct decisions, particularly with regard to life safety aspects of buildings. Certainly, it is important that the design function in a design-and-build contract is carried out by people with the knowledge and skills to ensure the design is safe and compliant with regulations and who also have the required professional liability insurance.

Table 12.1 A table discussing some of the issues related to cost, quality and time for the choice of contract types

Cost:		
Is it important to have the lowest cost?	Yes	A traditional contract will allow a fixed price if the design is fixed. Design-and-build will allow the contractor to design a cheaper building, so is appropriate if the design is not completed. A management contract can allow costs to be controlled.
	No	A traditional contract will give the greatest control of design and quality of construction, which may result in a higher price. A design-and-build contractor will charge a premium to take on design risk.
Is a fixed cost important?	Yes	If the design is fixed a traditional contract will give a fixed sum for the works. A design-and-build contract can include a fixed lump sum with the contractor taking on the risk of design changes for a premium.
	No	A traditional contract will include a mechanism to control costs where change is expected (e.g. on works to an existing building). A management contract will not give a confirmed cost until the last sub-contractor is appointed.
Quality:		
Is quality important?	Yes	A traditional contract will give the greatest control of design and quality of construction. Design and construction quality can be controlled also in a management arrangement.
	No	In a design-and-build contract control of quality is handed to the contractor. In a management arrangement the sub-contractors can have design responsibility similar to a design-and-build contract.
Time		
Does the client want the building built quickly?	Yes	A design-and-build contract allows the contractor to start on site whilst the design is being completed, thus shortening the overall project programme. A management contract allows the contract manager to tender works and even start on site before the design is completed, thus shortening the overall project programme.

(Continued)

Table 12.1 (Continued)

Cost:		
	No	In a traditional contract the design work should be completed before the works are tendered, making it likely the overall project programme will be longer.
Is a fixed contract period important?	Yes	A design-and-build contract can include a fixed contract period.
		The better the level of resolution of the design the more definite can be the contract period. If the design is well resolved in any contract form, the likelihood of extensions of time is reduced.
	No	The majority of contracts include an identified length of time for the contract.
		A management contract where the sub-contractors are not appointed and the design not resolved at appointment risks a longer contract period.

The contract form

The architect is recommended to use standard contract documents written by the Joint Contracts Tribunal (JCT) or other industry bodies, rather than one written specifically for the project by lawyers or others.

The Joint Contracts Tribunal is made up of members from across the building industry including private clients, local authorities, contractors, engineers, surveyors and the RIBA. The JCT contract is balanced between the different interests and is well known throughout the construction industry by providing a suite of different contracts for different purposes that have been developed and adapted by the JCT over many decades in response to changes to construction and the law around them. The JCT contracts can be bought from the RIBA or the JCT [1]. Figure 12.2 lists out the standard JCT contract forms.

The JCT forms are written for England and Wales. The Scottish Building Contracts Committee (SBCC) performs the same

Table 12.2 A table listing the JCT contract forms

Contract	Reference	Description
Standard Building Contract with Quantities	SBC/Q	A traditional contract suitable for a variety of project sizes. Where the building has been designed before tender. Includes for contractor design portions if required. Including measurement of the building and the creation of a Bill of Quantities (hence the term 'Quantities' in the title) by a quantity surveyor.
Standard Building Contract without Quantities	SBC/XQ	As for SBC/Q but with no measurement by a QS. The tender will be based on drawings and specifications from the design team.
Standard Building Contract with Approximate Quantities	SBC/AQ	As for SBC/Q but with approximate quantities.
Intermediate Building Contract	IC	A contract similar in form to SBC but for small to medium-sized projects, usually identified as ones where the construction period is a year or less. The contract costs can be a lump sum or measured as they proceed. This can be tendered on drawings and a bill of quantities, specifications or work schedules.
Intermediate Building Contract with Contractor's Design	ICD	As for IC but with contractor design portions.
Minor Works Building Contract	MW	A simpler form of traditional contract. Suitable for smaller residential and commercial projects. With no measurement by a quantity surveyor.
Minor Works Building Contract with Contractor's Design	MWD	As for MW but with contractor design portions.
Major Project Construction Contract	MP	A contract for major projects for clients who regularly carry out major works, which can be procured under a design-and-build arrangement and for contractors that are able to accept more risk.

(Continued)

Table 12.2 (Continued)

Contract	Reference	Description
Design-and-Build Contract	DB	A contract for design-and-build projects of varied sizes.
Management Building Contract	MC	A contract for projects where the main contractor appoints the sub-contractors and manages them for a fee.
Construction Management Appointment	CM/A	A contract for projects where the client appoints a contractor to manage the construction and the client also appoints all the trade contractors.
JCT Constructing Excellence Contract	CE	A contract for projects where the participants wish to work in a more co-operative way. The document can be used to procure a range of contract services.
Measured Term Contract	MTC	The Measured Term Contract is written for clients who wish to procure a series of maintenance or similar smaller works from a single contractor over a period.
Prime Cost Building Contract	PCC	A contract in a traditional, SBC, arrangement suitable for projects where the scope and design is not known at the start, for example reconstruction after fire damage, and the works can be measured and costed as they proceed.
Repair and Maintenance Contract	RM	A contract written for clients who regularly place maintenance work and don't have a contract administrator.
Building Contract and Consultancy Agreement for a Home Owner/ Occupier	HO/C and HO/CA	A simple traditional contract form with simple payment arrangements for a home owner who has appointed a consultant to design the project. There is an associated consultancy agreement (HO/CA) to go alongside the building contract (HO/C).
Building Contract for a Home Owner Occupier Who Has Not Appointed a Consultant to Oversee the Work	HO/B	As for HO/C for a home owner who has not appointed a design consultant.

Note: For each of the contract types the JCT also publishes users' guides and sub-contract forms.

function in Scotland [2]. Users in Northern Ireland should use the standard JCT forms, though there are some adaptations which can be obtained from the Royal Society of Ulster Architects [3].

There are other standard forms published by the Association of Consultant Architects (ACA), the Chartered Institute of Builders (CIOB), Institution of Civil Engineers who publish the New Engineering Contract (NEC) form, the RIBA who publish contracts for domestic and smaller commercial works, the Fédération Internationale des Ingénieurs-Conseils (FIDIC) who publish the FIDIC form, and on larger projects clients like to get their own bespoke forms written. By looking at the standard form the reader will understand how the contract works, and all variations of the terms in other forms can be comprehended by relating them back to the standard form.

Managing a construction contract

In this section we discuss some of the primary activities of managing a construction contract. The reader should also refer to Chapter 9 Project delivery where some of the issues arising during a project are described.

We will look at the standard Joint Contracts Tribunal 2016 form of contract, often called 'SBC 2016', as this is widely used for building projects, and is the RIBA's recommended form. This is a 'traditional' contract, which can form the basis of understanding the design-and-build, management and other forms. In contractual disputes the terms of SBC 2016 are taken to apply by the court if no other contract terms exist in the case.

We will not give commentary on every clause of the SBC2016 but restrict ourselves to discussing those areas that are normally contentious or difficult.

In Chapter 9 Project delivery, we discuss the items of work involved in setting up a project. We also set out the importance of clear and timely communication in the efficient and successful running of a project, and of recording that communication.

The 'CA' role

The SBC2016 refers to the 'Architect/Contract Administrator' and although these two roles are sometimes separated, we will refer to them as one, which we will call CA. The architect may find that someone else is appointed to the role of contract administrator – a client's representative, project manager or other – in which case the architect has no role in administering the contract. In this circumstance the architect's role is simply one of providing information for the design as described in the contract.

The CA role should be carried out accurately and in a timely fashion to ensure the project is delivered on time and on budget. The CA's role is to act on the employer's behalf quite literally to 'administer the building contract' and so will certify when works are completed, instruct variations, certify interim payments and monitor the progress of the works. However, an important point is that the CA must be impartial and unbiased in certifying interim payments, the valuations for which must be reasonable and justified and reflect the work carried out. The architect should study the contract carefully to ensure they understand fully their duties in managing the contract, and if there are points where the architect is unsure, they should be clarified.

Allowing for change

The primary cause of tension during construction is unexpected change – to the design, site, timing, market costs and so forth and coming from whatever source. Changes involve extra work, are likely to cost someone extra money and may delay completion of the building, so all the sources of potential change should be predicted wherever possible and allowed for in the project budget, the programme and the contract.

Contingencies and provisional sums

Elements of work that are either not yet designed or for some reason cannot be resolved can be allowed for in the cost plan as a contingency or provisional sum. Examples of items that might not be resolved are where a tenant or caterer has some input into the design, or where completion of the design is dependent on agreement with an adjoining owner. For items such as these a contingency allowance can be made in the budget based on an estimate of the likely work involved. When the element becomes resolved a change to the contract scope can be instructed.

Other items might not be resolved simply because although the scope is known the design is being left to later on; for example, if a special reception desk is to be included that will be drawn after the signature of the contract. In this case a 'provisional sum' can be included in the contract based on the expected sum to be spent on the desk. Elements of design might be left to later in the contract in this way either as the designer does not have sufficient resources earlier on or as the design of the element is dependent on decisions that will be made later in the programme.

Measurement and instructed changes

For a project where the overall scope of work cannot be clearly defined, for example works to an existing building where the full scope will only be known when construction work starts on site, a measurement contract form can be used. In this case rates are defined for different types of work and the regular payments are calculated on the measurement of the amount of work carried out. If a lump-sum contract form is used for such a project, the best estimate of the work can be made and a contingency allowance included in the client's budget with the knowledge that the figures included are only an estimate.

In Chapter 9 Project delivery, we set out a process for managing changes of design when they arise and include a typical change request form.

The SBC2016, and other contract forms, includes a mechanism for instructing changes to the design and to the programme, see 'Instructions' and 'Variations' next.

Instructions

SBC2016 clauses 3.10 to 3.22

Instructions can lead to Variations, see next, in which case the process described for Variations is recommended (see also Chapter 9 Project delivery, on management of changes). The contractor has the right to give reasonable objections to instructions that would lead to a Variation. An Instruction can lead to a Variation under clause 5.1, Definition of Variations, which can give the contractor the right to claim extra money under clause 4.20, Loss and Expense, and also give the contractor the right to claim additional time under clause 2.28, Fixing Completion Date.

Clause 3.12 allows for instructions to be given verbally where the process is that they have to be confirmed in writing either by the CA to the contractor or by the contractor to the CA, and in either case the instruction is only valid from the date of written confirmation. The written confirmation should be given as soon as possible and the author advises no later than within 24 hours. The contract allows seven days for the contractor's confirmation and then seven days for the CA to dissent. As a rule, verbal instructions are to be avoided as they tend to be given without sight of the documentation and they risk being forgotten or misunderstood.

Clause 3.18 allows the CA to instruct work to be removed if it is built not in accordance with the contract and the contractor cannot claim additional money or time for this work. The CA can also instruct areas to be opened up to see if work has been constructed in compliance with the contract documents, but this can be a gamble as the contractor has the right to claim for additional time on the programme, and additional money under clause 4.22.2, if the work was in fact built correctly.

For clarity, all items for which the contractor claims a Variation should be the subject of an Instruction if they are valid.

Variations

SBC2016 clauses 5.1 to 5.10

A Variation as defined in clause 5.1 Definition of Variations is firstly the addition, omission or change of any of the work, or secondly the change of the conditions of the site or pro-gramme, and is likely to allow the contractor to claim for additional monies under clause 5.3 or 2.29.1, and possibly additional time – see later The process of extensions of time. Clause 4.22.3 allows the contractor to claim additional costs to comply with instructions that rectify discrepancies in the contract documents. It has been the author's experience that sometimes architects have not fully documented part of the design at tender stage, then have issued more drawings show-ing more detail after signature of the contract only to find the contractor claiming additional monies for what the architect thought was simply a clarification of a design that was already established. To avoid this situation architects should be careful to ensure that their design is fully communicated at tender stage.

Clause 5.3 sets out a process whereby the CA can request a written Variation Quotation from the contractor and can then accept it by issue of a Confirmed Acceptance, or preferably an Instruction.

Contractors are paid for Variations through the monthly pay-ment certificate process.

Change control

A clear change control process is vital to every project of any size so that each suggested change can be tracked and recorded. This should start, before the change is instructed, with a process that identifies the cost and programme effects of the proposed change so that the implications can be clearly understood. A form such as that illustrated in Chapter 9 Project delivery, Figure 9.7 and discussed in the accompanying text will assist with the management of this. Time is of great importance in the management of changes, particularly once construction has started, so any analysis and discussion of a proposed change should be within time limits agreed with the contractor.

Adjustment of the completion date

SBC2016 clauses 2.26 to 2.29

The CA can instruct a new completion date if they receive a notice of delay from the contractor and are of the opinion the works will be delayed due to a Relevant Event. Clause 2.29 lists the Relevant Events which give the contractor cause to request additional time on the contract including (for the full list see SBC2016):

- Variations;
- Other instructions as listed, including the opening up of works to confirm their compliance with the contract unless they are found to be non-compliant;
- Any impediment to the contractor's works by the client or CA;
- Works by statutory undertakers (installers of gas, electricity, water supply, drainage, telecoms);
- Exceptionally adverse weather conditions;
- Lightning strikes, floods and the like;
- Civil commotion or strikes;

- Government action;
- A named specialist becoming insolvent;
- Force majeure.

It should be noted that 'exceptionally adverse weather conditions', which is not normal wind or rain that the contractor should allow for, is not defined in the standard contract. It can be helpful to define it, for example the NEC defines it as weather over a calendar month that occurs less often than once in ten years. The weather on site can be recorded to assist in clarity of this matter.

The process of extensions of time

As soon as the contractor becomes aware the work is being delayed or likely to be delayed, they should give a notice to the CA identifying the cause of the delay referring to clause 2.29, Relevant Events, and giving the expected period of delay. The CA then assesses the notice and can issue an Instruction for a new completion date. The architect may judge that the delay is not due to Relevant Events, or only partly due to them, in which case they can instruct a new date that is not the one suggested by the contractor.

If the actual completion date is after the contract completion date the employer can claim Liquidated and Ascertained Damages from the contractor under clause 2.32, provided they have given notice in advance of the Final Certificate that they intend to do this.

Payments SBC2016 clauses 4.8 to 4.15, Interim Payments, and 4.26, Final Certificate and final payment

The CA approves monthly valuations for payments to the contractor, called Interim Payments, and the Final Payment at the end of the project. For Interim Payments the process described is that the contractor issues a Payment Application to the quantity surveyor who assesses the amount due, then the CA issues an Interim Payment Certificate to the contractor.

Interim Certificates should include for work completed on site, but only if it is correct. If there is any question about whether the work is built correctly in accordance with the drawings and specification, or whether the quality of the construction is suitable, it should not be included. Materials delivered to site can be included, though clause 4.14.1.2 makes it clear they must be protected against weather and damage and must not have been delivered to site prematurely. Materials off site may also be included in the valuation, but the conditions for their inclusion, set out in clause 4.16 Listed Items, are stringent: the goods must be clearly identified as ordered by the client, for the project; proof must be given that they are owned by the contractor and they must be covered by insurance to their full value. If it has been specifically identified in the contract the contractor must also provide a bond for such goods.

The reader's attention is drawn to clause 4.22 setting out the Relevant Matters giving the contractor valid cause to claim additional monies including for instructions and variations.

Completion

SBC2016 clauses 2.30 to 2.39
When, in the CA's opinion, the contractor has completed the works, or a section of the works if partial completion was agreed, they can issue a Practical Completion Certificate. If the works are not complete on the relevant contract Completion Date, the architect should issue a Non-Completion Certificate.

At Practical Completion the ownership of the building is handed back to the client who then takes over insurance and management of it, and is able to occupy it.

At the issue of the Practical Completion Certificate the Recti-fication Period, or 'defects liability period' starts. This defaults to six months if another period is not identified in the contract and is commonly a year for larger projects. At the end of the Rectification Period the architect makes a list of all the defects on site due to the original construction, not any wear and tear that has occurred due to usage of the building. This must be issued within 14 days and the contractor then has a reasonable period, to be agreed, in which to rectify the defects.

When this is done the architect issues a Certificate of Making Good of defects which leads to the issue of a Final Certificate of payment. A retention is withheld for the rectification of defects that is then paid in the Final Certificate.

References

[1] The Joint Contracts Tribunal. www.jctltd.co.uk
[2] The Scottish Building Contracts Committee. www.sbcconline.com
[3] The Royal Society of Ulster Architects. www.rsua.org.uk

13
Quality assurance

Introduction

Quality assurance (QA) is primarily an idea of establishing a set of processes in the office in a quality management system (QMS) to ensure a good-quality product is consistently delivered.

For architects, these processes involve checking that all information issued from the architect's office meets regulatory standards, the project requirements and office expectations, and then documenting that the checks have been completed. The QA processes should be described in a manual and then there should be records that they have been carried out on each occasion.

Such a QA system gives confidence to various outside parties that the product will be reliably of good quality. Clients notably will be assured that their building will be of a consistent standard and that it has been checked. However, it can also help architects in maintaining consistency in their processes and output and, if followed correctly, provide a way of improving these.

Some clients may want to see proof of the QA system, and some larger organisations will only want to employ companies that are certified under ISO 9001, Quality Management Systems [1]. Professional indemnity insurers may also want to have sight of QA systems or QA certification.

Advantages of having an office QMS are:

- Improved quality of the product issued from the office and therefore of the projects built;

DOI: 10.4324/9781003327288-16

- Client confidence;
- Efficiency can be improved by establishing a systematic approach to work in the office;
- Therefore improved profitability.
- Reliable office systems can also improve staff confidence and morale.

The core of quality assurance is a checking process on all drawings, reports, presentations and other information before they leave the office. Everyone in the office must know what the processes are and must be able to see they are being followed.

The process of quality assurance is sometimes described as 'plan, do, check, act'. These four actions can be applied either to the QA processes or to the carrying out of design work.

In the author's view all time spent on planning out the work to be done is time well spent.

The office manual and office quality manual

The starting point is to document the office processes in an Office Manual. The Office Manual is sometimes separate from the Office Quality Manual if the latter is just describing the quality management processes. The Office Manual should primarily describe the processes around running a project but should also cover all the other activities in the office such as

Table 13.1 The 'plan, do check, act' processes

	QA process	Design work
Plan	Design the processes	Plan out the design work
Do	Implement the processes	Carry out the design work
Check	Review the processes	Check the work to ensure the design is correct
Act	Amend the processes where the review found deficiencies	Amend the design where any errors or discrepancies are found

hiring staff, managing communications and so on. This should include the processes themselves and any standard forms, databases, software and the like that are part of the process.

Table 13.2 illustrates a suggested list of office processes to be included in an Office Manual.

Table 13.2 A table listing out suggested contents for an Office Manual

Process	Accompanying standard forms and policies
Project acquisition	
Business development	Record of potential opportunities
Initial proposal	Proposal standard format
Project start-up	
Setting up a project within the office:	Project Quality Plan
	Project filing structure
Project proposal	Project programme
	Project staffing plan
	Project fees workplan
	An offer letter to a client
	A larger brochure-style project proposal
The architect's appointment	The RIBA Standard Professional Services Contract [2]
	Shortened forms of letters of appointment,
The appointment of a sub-consultant to the architect	A sub-consultant appointment
Drawing standards	
Setting up a project on the office drawing platform	File structure, level structure, standard elements, references, etc.
The importing and checking of other consultants' information	Consultants' drawing register Standard comment form
The drawings of building elements	Standard office methods for drawing buildings and parts of buildings
Setting up drawings	Office drawing frames for large and small drawings and sketches
	Standard setting out of buildings and elements on a drawing
Issuing drawings; processes for checking the information before issue and for the recording of issue	Drawing checking forms Drawing register and issue forms
BIM	BIM standards

(Continued)

Table 13.2 (Continued)

Process	Accompanying standard forms and policies
Project design	
Briefing	Briefing forms
	Brief brochure
Stages	Model project stage design reports
Planning	A model Design and Access Statement
Client sign-off	Standard letter or form requesting a client sign-off
Commenting on other consultants' information	Consultants' drawing register
	Standard comment form
Project delivery (see also Chapter 9 Project delivery)	
Project management handbook	Containing the forms listed here
Project execution plan	Model project execution plan
Project meetings	Meeting minutes
The management of change	Variation request form (see Chapter 9 Figure 9.10)
The management of the relationship with the contractor	Request for Information form
Management of the contract (see also Chapter 12 Building contracts) Notices, certificates and instructions are referred to in the SBC 2016 Items marked 'JCT' are standard forms available from the JCT	Information Release Schedule
	Confirmed Acceptance (of a variation quotation or an acceleration quotation)
	Instruction (JCT) by the Contract Administrator or Architect
	Pay Less Notice
	Interim Certificate (Payment Certificate) (JCT)
	Statement of Retention (JCT)
	Statement of Reimbursement of Advance Payment (JCT)
	Notice of Partial Possession by the Employer (JCT)
	Notice of Adjustment of Completion Date (JCT)
	Non-Completion Certificate (JCT)
	Section Completion Certificate (JCT)
	Practical Completion Certificate (JCT)
	Certificate of Making Good (JCT)
	Final Certificate (Payment Certificate) (JCT)

(Continued)

Table 13.2 (Continued)

Process	Accompanying standard forms and policies
Site management	Site observation form
Defects inspection	Defects recording forms or database
Completion	Health and Safety File
	Operation and Maintenance manual
	Building User's Guide
Recording and filing the	Project filing form
project information	Project drawings files for easy reference
In use	
In use survey	Client in use feedback form
Office management	
Invoicing	Invoice
Monthly reporting	Monthly report
Annual reporting	Annual report for internal use
	Annual report to issue to Companies House
Yearly forecast	12-month forecast
	3- or 5-year forecast
Accounts	Accountancy procedures
Board meeting	Board reports
	Meeting minutes
Environmental management	Environmental Management policy
Health and Safety	Health and Safety policy
Staff	
Interviewing and appointing	Employment policy
employees	
	Equality, Diversity and Inclusion policy
	Staff interview format
Briefing a new staff member	Guide to briefing a new employee
Professional development and	CPD and training policy
training	

Project execution plan

The information and processes for each project can then be set out in a project execution plan (PEP), see Chapter 9 Project delivery.

Quality management systems (QMS)

RIBA Chartered Practices are required to have a minimum quality management system appropriate to the size of the practice:

Small practices (1 to 10 staff): the RIBA Project Quality Plan for Small Projects or equivalent should be used on all projects.

Medium-sized practices (11 to 50 staff): the RIBA Quality Management Toolkit [3] should be used on all projects and for the office procedures.

Larger practices (51 or more staff): the practice should have a quality management system certified under BS EN ISO 9001: 2015 Quality Management Systems – Requirements [1]. ISO 9001 is a globally recognised standard for quality management. It helps organisations of all sizes and sectors to improve their performance, meet customer expectations and demonstrate their commitment to quality. Its requirements define how to establish, implement, maintain and continually improve a quality management system. Note that the standard is generic so architectural practices will have to develop their own appropriate process based on its principles. Specialist companies will consult on the system and then provide external certification, which is normally renewed every three years. External certification is not a requirement. The systems can be based on the RIBA Quality Management Toolkit or on another externally certified system or they can be developed internally to achieve certification.

References

[1] ISO 9001:2015. Quality Management Systems, Requirements. www.iso.org
[2] Standard Professional Services Contract 2020. London: RIBA Publishing.
[3] RIBA Chartered Practice Quality Management System. https://www.architecture.com/knowledge-and-resources/resources-landing-page/chartered-practice-toolbox

14
Computing

Introduction

Computing systems are the foundations of modern architectural practice, as they are for many businesses today. Above the operating systems such as Microsoft Windows OS, Apple OS or Linux OS programmes can be split into two broad categories – those for production of drawings or written material and those for management and accounts. These two categories of systems do not generally link across to each other.

The office computing set-up should be designed for flexibility – to allow people to work from the office, from home, or on the road; to allow the office to expand quickly if a new project demands it; to integrate with new software if a new system is available or if a client requests working on a specific platform.

This book is written at a time when AI is beginning to be used in architecture. It is assisting in the design process with images and design development, and it is being used in writing. This technology is new to architecture and will not be discussed in detail here. The reader is urged to keep abreast of this subject as it develops.

Hardware

The author will not say much here about hardware and will leave the reader to select the computers, screens and other equipment most suitable to their size of office, their projects and their way of working. His experience has shown that reliability is a quality that should be prioritised in the selection of equipment as IT failures can be very disruptive.

DOI: 10.4324/9781003327288-17

Note that software packages will require certain hardware capacity to run them, and some software programmes are specific about their requirements. This should be a key factor when selecting computer hardware. If in doubt conduct tests or contact a technology expert before making a final decision.

Storage and backup

Storage on the cloud is the best current practice as it allows files to be accessed from any location, and it is more secure than having storage in the office. There are many providers of online storage, some of whom offer other services, such as website hosting.

'Cloud' storage is hosted in data centres which generally have backup power and are physically secure, so data is unlikely to be lost from them. However, some companies prefer also to have their data backed up on their own storage system kept either in the office, if this is sufficiently secure, or at a remote secure location. In these circumstances the data should be backed up at least weekly so that the maximum amount of work that would have to be re-done in case of loss is seven days' worth.

Some thoughts about data backups

The 3–2-1 backup rule: this rule suggests having three total copies of data, two of which are local but on different devices, and one copy off site. This approach protects against data loss in almost any scenario. Regularly schedule backups: automated backups occurring at regular intervals ensure that the most recent data is always backed up without having to remember to do it manually. Test the backups: regularly test the backups to verify that the data can be restored. This testing helps identify potential issues before the office is in a situation where it needs to rely on the backed-up data.

Security

The IT systems need to be protected against bad actors trying to damage the system or steal from the company or its employees. This is partly a matter of having security software to counter viruses that is kept up to date. Norton [1] and McAfee [2] are leading anti-virus software producers, and there are many other good systems available. Note however the users are probably the weakest part of any system as bad actors currently try to enter systems through contact with the users by email or phone to get information or money. All users need to be vigilant of potential threats, such as emails from unknown sources asking the recipient to click on a link, and therefore need to be informed of how these threats are changing with time.

Business continuation

As well as potential threats to the IT system, the business can be put at risk by physical disruption occurring from threats such as floods, fires or burglary that can put the office or its people out of action. The practice should have a plan that will enable it to continue to operate if, for example, there is a complete power outage that makes the office unusable.

The plan should identify:

• Alternative staffing arrangements if there is a risk some of the staff may not be able to work. This might be a re-allocation of work with the current people, or the acquisition of temporary staff to cover;
• Alternative office accommodation, which might be for staff to work from home;
• IT arrangements that will allow the office to function at the alternative office location;
• Alternative communications arrangements, such as for the office phone number, and communications between staff when they are in the temporary location;

- Meetings. Arrangements to host internal and external meetings, online or in person.

An office can be kept running during a short power outage by having an uninterruptable power supply, called UPS, which is a battery that comes into operation immediately after the mains power is lost. The UPS for a large office can be bulky and attract ongoing power and ventilation costs. To keep running during longer power outages would require an alternative power supply such as generators that come on when mains power fails. The UPS can be used to cover the period when the mains power has failed and the generator is starting up. Although the author has designed buildings with backup generators, he has not heard of an architect's office in the United Kingdom with such a system.

Generally a practice with all its IT storage online will enable the staff to work from home or an alternative office. To make this workable all paper documents in the office that are needed for the business must be also in an electronic form. Thus, all drawings, letters or other printed material arriving as paper copies should be scanned or received in parallel as PDF or other electronic versions.

Staff should also not store important business information on their laptops as these can be broken or stolen, even if they never leave the office.

Production systems

Introduction

The production systems should be appropriate to the size and complexity of the projects the practice is working on just as the management systems should be appropriate to the size of the office. More sophisticated systems may involve the practice in more work than is necessary to produce the design information, and in more time and money spent on management, on staff and on software than it can afford. Using the simplest system appropriate to the work will keep down production costs and overheads.

The production systems are part of the overall reputation and make-up of the practice on offer to clients. The government, for example, requires projects to be developed on BIM, so to bid for these the office will need to have the software, staff skills and production systems to handle BIM.

Architects known to the author find they can work most efficiently with the software they know, so their choice of software will be influenced by what they are used to.

The author recommends all architects should be able to sketch by hand to create convincing images of their ideas at the initial stages of a project and to develop ideas for construction details. There is various software for sketching in 2D and 3D on laptops, tablets and mobile phones, some of which enable the sketch to be converted to dimensioned information.

Modelling packages, for example Rhino [3] and SketchUp [4], can be used to develop a concept, and when this is agreed it can then be moved to Revit [5] or other BIM software to develop the production information. This can be the most time-efficient method as the BIM model can take more time to establish and to manipulate than to design using the sketching software.

Developing production information in BIM can save time as co-ordination internally and with other consultants can be easier, all the production information is in one place, and manufacturers and suppliers commonly issue 3D models of their products that can be placed in the BIM model.

Building information modelling (BIM)

The term BIM describes a process for creating, specifying and managing digital information about a built asset. This is a system whereby the building is designed as a 3D model. The model can contain information from surveys, the architect, the various engineering disciplines, the contractors and sub-contractors and anyone else who needs to contribute. The architectural information can include specification clauses or links across to a specification document, and the outputs can include production drawings; acoustic, thermal, structural calculations; area schedules; manufacturing schedules; and facilities management information for the end user.

The Government Construction Strategy published in May 2011 stated that all centrally procured government construction projects would be required to be developed in fully collaborative 3D BIM from April 2016, called 'level 2 BIM'. This relates to the definition of the sophistication of the use of CAD:

Level 0: represents unmanaged CAD (computer-aided design).
Level 1: represents managed CAD in 2D or 3D.
Level 2: represents managed 3D environment with data attached, but created in separate discipline models.
Level 3: represents single, online, project model with construction sequencing, cost and lifecycle management information.

The standard governing BIM for the design phase of buildings is ISO 19650 part 2 2018 'Organization and digitization of information about buildings and civil engineering works, including building information modelling (BIM) – Information management using building information modelling Part 2: Delivery phase of the assets'.

Part 1 is Concepts and Principles;
Part 3 is Operational Phase of the Assets;
Part 4 is Information Exchange;
Part 5 is Security-Minded Approach to Management.

The former standards BS 1192 2007 +A2 and Publicly Available Specification (PAS) 1192–2 2013 were superseded by ISO 19650.

Guidance about national BIM standards can be found at UK BIM Framework [6] run by BSI and NIMA, a voluntary association of organisations promoting BIM usage. This gives standards, guidance and resources which constitute the overarching approach to information management using BIM in the UK. It is based on ISO 19650 and is updated regularly.

When setting up a project that will be developed using BIM, an Information Protocol, or 'BIM Execution Plan', should be established. This should set out:

• What software will be used by all the different parties on the project. These will all need to be compatible.
• When and how information will be exchanged between the parties. It is normal during the design stages for information to be co-ordinated at regular intervals, perhaps fortnightly, and before submissions or presentations. Note that the co-ordination issue will need to take place some days or even weeks before a deadline to allow clashes and co-ordination issues to be found and resolved.
• Who will manage the co-ordination of the information from the different parties. This person might be called the BIM manager for the project.
• What level of detail (LOD) will be achieved at each stage of the project. See also Chapter 9 Project delivery for a discussion of the design completeness at RIBA stages and the relationship with BIM LOD.

The three-dimensional model of the building can either consist in a series of models developed separately by each of the parties, architects and engineers (level 2 BIM), or it can be a single 'federated model' held centrally that all the parties can work on simultaneously (level 3 BIM). If the project is set up with separated models then the management of the co-ordination of the models needs to be set out in the BIM Execution Plan. A federated model can be hosted centrally through software such as Autodesk's BIM 360 cloud.

Levels of detail (LOD) for BIM were developed by the American Institute of Architects and so relate to the United States project stages. See Chapter 9 Project delivery for a comparison of some international definitions of project work stages:

LOD 100 describes concept design stages, essentially the equivalent of hand-sketched or symbolic digital 2D representations of the project.

LOD 200 describes the schematic design stage where a partially defined idea with approximate project sizing, form and building elements are established.

LOD 300 describes the detail stage of a project whereby a 3D digital model represents the building in terms of architectural design and engineering drawings with more exact localised dimensions and elements.

LOD 350 is a halfway stage between detailing and fabrication, a point where tools such as clash detection are employed to ensure individual elements are synchronised into the whole, resolving co-ordination issues and inconsistencies to produce a construction-ready model.

LOD 400 is the last stage of modelling before fabrication and assembly. The model must contain an accurate representation of the elements, objects and thus building with finalised and defined elements, sizes, locations, connections, materials and so on.

LOD 500 represents the as-built final model of the building with supplementary information such as installation processes, installation dates, comments on issues, notes for the users and so on.

Some popular programmes for architectural design are:

Autodesk Revit [5] – Widely used for BIM, Revit also supports high-quality rendering and integrates well with other visualisation tools.

Bentley MicroStation [7] – a 2D and 3D drawing and package that can be used for BIM.

Autodesk 3ds Max [8] – Known for its powerful 3D modelling capabilities, 3ds Max is frequently used for rendering and creating detailed animations in architecture.

SketchUp [4] – Popular for its user-friendly interface, SketchUp is great for 3D modelling and comes with an extensive library of models and plugins.

Rhinoceros (Rhino) [3] – Renowned for its mathematical precision in 3D modelling, Rhino is used for complex architectural forms and integrates with various rendering plugins like V-Ray.

Lumion [9] – Known for its ability to produce high-quality renders quickly, Lumion is favoured for creating videos and real-time 3D architectural visualisations.

V-Ray [10] – A good-quality software for rendering in multiple architectural software platforms, V-Ray is known for its high-quality outputs and realistic light simulations.

Blender [11] – An open-source 3D modelling and rendering software getting known amongst architects for its powerful suite of tools that include animation.

ArchiCAD [12] – A BIM-focused software that offers robust tools for modelling and rendering, widely used by architects for its intuitive design capabilities and good integration with various rendering engines.

Cinema 4D [13] – Often used for motion graphics, Cinema 4D also offers excellent capabilities for architectural visualisations, rendering and 3D modelling.

Enscape [14] – A real-time rendering and virtual reality plugin that works with software like Revit, SketchUp and Rhino to create immersive architectural visualisations.

Visualisation software

The architect will want to present his or her work through images and perhaps videos and interactive models. For this he or she may be able to produce models through SketchUp or Rhino that will be presentable. For more sophisticated, realistic presentations, images from modelling software will need to be developed in presentation programmes such as Adobe Photoshop.

Physical models can be produced from 3D computer models either through 3D printing or through the production of the elements of a physical model from the CAD data.

Virtual reality (VR)

Increasingly architects are presenting their designs using virtual reality (VR), a 3D computer model presented primarily through a headset with two small screens, one for each eye, giving 3D vision as the user moves around the building. This allows architects to better understand their designs and therefore to solve problems that are not so easy to see in other presentations. It also allows the design to be communicated more successfully to non-technical people and is a more impressive way for a client to view the building design. Overall, VR's immersive experience improves traditional architectural practices, leading to more effective communication, efficient design development, and ultimately, superior architectural outcomes.

Management and accounts systems

There are software packages available for most aspects of management of the architects' office, as described next. Some of these packages will link across to each other and some will not. If the user wants their systems to integrate together they should investigate how they will work together before investing time and money in them.

Unless accounts are going to be managed manually or on a spreadsheet, the architectural practice will require accounts software. There are many programmes targeted at the small business or people starting a new business such as Xero [15], QuickBooks [16], Sage [17] and FreeAgent [18]. All of these will manage money in and money out and VAT and they will produce reports. Using software can save time over manual accounts by automating invoicing, identifying VAT and performing other tasks.

These programmes have additional plug-ins to manage projects, international currencies and staff payroll and have other features, for which there may be an additional cost. Refer to the websites of the software companies to see what each one offers.

Timesheets

Some of these accounting software packages include additional functionality to manage staff timesheets and then allocate their costs against projects. 'Timesheet Portal' [19] is a package for timesheet management that plugs in to standard accounting software. Alternatively, timesheets can be managed through a project management programme such as those mentioned in the following section which can then link across to the accounting software.

Project management software

Additional to accounting software are packages that centre on the management of projects. In these the architect can identify the tasks involved in a project including how long they will take, allocate staff to them, add expenses and obtain a cost for the work. This can be done when bidding for a project, and then the software can be used to manage the profitability of the project as it progresses. The information can be used to see the overall current workload and future workload for the company.

CMap [20] is such a project management software specifically designed for services companies including architects. Other similar software packages are Harvest [21], Scoro [22], Monday.com [23] and Asana [24]. All of these will link across to accounting software such as Xero. Deltek [25] can manage accounts, projects, staff and CRM.

Programming or scheduling software

To plan out the timescale of a project, as discussed in Chapter 9 Project delivery, the architect will need to draw a programme, also called a schedule. The author has used Microsoft Project which has sufficient functionality for the normal drawing of programmes for architectural projects. This software can include staff allocated against tasks, identify costs and be used to track progress during the lifetime of the project. Other programming software packages have similar functionality, for example GanttPRO [26] and Portfolio Manager [27].

Many major construction companies use Primavera P6 [28], a sophisticated database-based programming software that is probably more complicated than most architects will require for their own work, though they may encounter it in use by contractors.

Client relationship management (CRM)

Other software can assist with the management of relationships with contacts and potential clients. These can record contact information, activities and communications with people and organisations. Note the European GDPR sets limitations on how much information about people can be stored, which is discussed in Chapter 5 Marketing and business development.

Deltek [25], primarily an accounting software, can also keep track of interactions with contacts and potential clients. There are many sophisticated CRM software packages available, the majority of them aimed at industries where the pursuit of multiple clients is a more central part of the activity of the companies than it generally is for architects.

Human resources (HR)

There are software packages available to manage staff – with an employee database that can produce reports, payroll, time and benefits, hiring and introduction to the company (called 'onboarding'). Some packages come as a subscription with experienced HR advice as part of the package. An example of this is BambooHR [29].

What IT does a start-up office require?
The author would recommend the following software as a minimum for an architect's office starting out with a workload of smaller projects:

MS Office.

A drawing package. A purely 2D package may be sufficient for smaller projects. A simpler, and therefore cheaper, package that can handle 3D design might be required. A company starting out will only need to invest in software that can handle BIM if it has the projects and income to justify it.

Visualisation software such as Adobe Acrobat, Photoshop and InDesign [30] to produce images and reports.

Accounts software. Note that many accounts software packages offer a 'starter package'.

The office will need to buy a storage mechanism, cloud storage for example, and hosting for its website.

References

[1] Norton. https://uk.norton.com
[2] McAfee. https://www.mcafee.com
[3] Rhino: Rhinoceros by Robert McNeel and Associates (TLM, Inc.). www.rhino3d.com
[4] SketchUp: SketchUp by Trimble. https://www.sketchup.com
[5] Revit. https://www.autodesk.co.uk/products/revit/
[6] UK BIM Framework. https://ukbimframework.org
[7] Bentley MicroStation. https://www.bentley.com/software/microstation/
[8] Autodesk 3ds Max. https://www.autodesk.co.uk/products/3ds-max/
[9] Lumion. https://lumion.com

[10] V-Ray. https://www.chaos.com/3d-rendering-software
[11] Blender. https://www.blender.org
[12] ArchiCAD. https://www.graphisoft.com/solutions/archicad/
[13] Cinema 4D. https://www.maxon.net/en/cinema-4d/
[14] Enscape. https://enscape3d.com
[15] Xero. https://www.xero.com
[16] QuickBooks. https://quickbooks.intuit.com
[17] Sage. https://www.sage.com
[18] FreeAgent. https://www.freeagent.com
[19] Timesheet Portal. https://www.timesheetportal.com
[20] CMap. https://www.cmap.io
[21] Harvest. https://www.getharvest.com
[22] Scoro. https://www.scoro.com
[23] Monday.com. https://monday.com
[24] Asana. https://asana.com
[25] Deltek. https://www.deltek.com
[26] GanttPRO. https://ganttpro.com
[27] Portfolio Manager by Tempo, formerly called Liquid Planner. https://www.liquidplanner.com
[28] Primavera P6. https://www.oracle.com/uk/construction-engineering/primavera-P6/
[29] BambooHR. https://www.bamboohr.com/g2/
[30] Adobe. https://www.adobe.com

Bibliography

Alford, S. and Tricker, R. 2023. *Building Regulations Pocket Book*, 2nd ed. London: Abingdon, Oxfordshire.

Bielefeld, B., Schneider, R., Brandt, T. and Franssen, S. 2013. *Basics Project Management, Architecture*. Basel, Switzerland: Birkhauser.

Brindley, R. 2022. *Good Practice Guide, Professionalism at Work*. London: RIBA Publishing.

Brookhouse, S. 2020. *Part 3 Handbook*, 4th ed. London: RIBA Publishing.

Chappell, D. and Dunn, M. H. 2016. *The Architect in Practice*, 11th ed. London: Wiley Blackwell.

Charlson, J. and Dimka, N. 2024. *Lessons from Grenfell Tower, The New Building Safety Regime*. London: Abingdon, Oxfordshire.

Cousins, N. 2020. *Architect's Legal Pocket Book*. London: Abingdon, Oxfordshire.

Eastman, C., Teicholz, P., Sachs, R. and Liston, K. 2018. *BIM Handbook: A Guide to Building Information Modelling for Owners, Designers, Engineers, Contractors and Facility Managers*, 3rd ed. New Jersey: John Wiley and Sons Ltd.

Egan, J. 1998. *Rethinking Construction: Report of the Construction Task Force*. London: HMSO.

Egan, J. 2002. *Accelerating Change: Consultation Paper by Strategic Forum for Construction*. London: HMSO.

Farrall, P. and Brookhouse, S. 2021. *Good Practice Guide: Fees*. London: RIBA Publishing.

Fewings, P. and Henjewele, C. 2019. *Construction Project Management, an Integrated Approach*, 3rd ed. London: Abingdon, Oxfordshire.

Hackitt, D. J. 2018. *Building a Safer Future, Independent Review of Building Regulations and Fire Safety: Final Report*. London: HMSO.

Haylock, C. 2021. *Good Practice Guide, Making Successful Planning Applications*. London: RIBA Publishing.

Howarth, T. and Greenwood, D. 2017. *Construction Quality Management, Principles and Practice*, 2nd ed. London: Abingdon, Oxfordshire.

Joint Contracts Tribunal. 2019. *BIM and JCT Contracts*. London: Sweet and Maxwell Ltd.

Kaye, B. 1960. *The Development of the Architectural Profession in Britain*. London: George Allen and Unwin Ltd.

Kemp, M. 2022. *Good Practice Guide, Business Resilience*. London: RIBA Publishing.

Knikker, J. 2021. *How to Win Work: The Architect's Guide to Business Development and Marketing*. London: RIBA Publishing.

Latham, M. 1994. *Constructing the Team*. London: HMSO.

Morrell, P. and Day, A. 2023. *Testing for a Safer Future, an Independent Review of the Construction Products Testing Regime*. London: DLUHC.

National Audit Office Report. 2005. Using Modern Methods of Construction to Build Homes More Quickly and Efficiently. https://www.nao.org.uk/uploads/2005/11/mmc.pdf

Nelson, C., Nuttall, G., Ronco, W., Beveridge, J. and Reigle, J. 2017. *Managing Quality in Architecture: Integrating BIM, Risk and Design Process*, 2nd ed. London: Abingdon, Oxfordshire.

Ostime, N. 2017. *A Commercial Client's Guide to Engaging an Architect*. London: RIBA Publishing.

Ostime, N. 2017. *A Domestic Client's Guide to Engaging an Architect*. London: RIBA Publishing.

Ostime, N. 2020. *RIBA Job Book*. London: RIBA Publishing.

Ostime, N. 2021. *Small Projects Handbook*, 2nd ed. London: RIBA Publishing.

Peterson, G., Kouider, T. and Paterson, G. 2015. *Getting to Grips with BIM, a Guide for Small and Medium-Sized Architecture, Engineering and Construction Firms*. London: Abingdon, Oxfordshire.

Race, S. 2013. *BIM Demystified*, 2nd ed. London: RIBA Publishing.

Shepherd, D. 2015. *The BIM Management Handbook*. London: NBS and RIBA Enterprises.

Speight, K. C. A. and Thorne, M. 2021. *Architect's Legal Handbook: the Law for Architects*. London: Abingdon, Oxfordshire.

Thompson, M. 2024. *Handbook of Practice Management*, 10th ed. London: RIBA Publishing.

Walker, A. 2015. *Project Management in Construction*, 6th ed. London: Wiley Blackwell.

Wevill, J. 2018. *Law in Practice: The RIBA Legal Handbook*. 3rd ed. London: RIBA Publishing.

Index

Note: Page numbers in *italics* indicate figures, and page numbers in **bold** indicate tables in the text

3–2–1 backup rule 218

accounts 41, 83–85; software 226, 229
accruals 84; basis 94
advertisements 52, 60
agency 60; recruitment 60–61
alternative method of compliance, Building Regulations 176
Ancient Monuments and Archaeological Areas Act (1979) 178
ancillary buildings 179
annual reports 86
appeals, planning 169
approval process: in England and Wales 181–182; in Northern Ireland 185; in Scotland 184
Approved Documents 176
ArchiCAD 225
architect 15–16; appointment 113–117; with technical knowledge and design skills 44
Architects Act (1997) 17–20, 40
Architects (Registration) Act (1931) 17
Architect's Legal Handbook 31, 115
Architect's Legal Pocket Book 39, 115, 137
The Architects Registration Board (ARB) 15, 16–18, 116

Architects Registration Council of the UK (ARCUK) 17
architectural practice 1; forms of 19–23; legal structures of 19; naming of 40–41; setting up (*see* starting an architectural practice); strategic description 29; structure of 31–40
asset lock 37
Autodesk 3ds Max 225
Autodesk Revit 224
Autumn Budget (2017) 7

BambooHR 229
B Corporations 23
Bentley MicroStation 224
bespoke contract 115; *see also* contracts
bias, employment 61
bidding for work 54
BIM *see* building information modelling (BIM)
Blender 225
brand 46
brief 122–123, 132–133, *134*
brochures 50–51
Building Act (1984) 175
building contracts *see* contracts
building control 175; approval with full plans 181–182; dispensations and relaxations 180–181; process of 179–181

Building Control Approver 156, 180, 181

Building Design and Construction 103–104

building information modelling (BIM) 221–222; ArchiCAD 225; Autodesk 3ds Max 225; Autodesk Revit 224; Bentley MicroStation 224; Blender 225; Cinema 4D 225; Enscape 225; Execution Plan 223; levels of detail (LOD) 223–224; Lumion 225; Rhinoceros (Rhino) 225; SketchUp 225; V-Ray 225

Building Notice procedure 181

Building Regulations 156, 175–178; application 181; dispensations and relaxations 180–181; in England and Wales 181–182; exemptions from 179; Hackitt's suggestion 9; in Northern Ireland 185

Building Research Establishment Environmental Assessment Method (BREEAM) 101–103, **102**

Building Safety Act 10–12, 156, 157, 180, 182–184

Building Safety Regulator (BSR) 10, 156, 168, 180, 182–183

buildings safety, golden thread 9

building standards application: in Northern Ireland 185; in Scotland 184

Building User's Guide 157

Building Warrant 184

building work 179–180

business continuation 219–220

business development 43; costs 53; planning 45, 46–47, 53–54

business plan, for new venture 28–30; and financial forecast 30; financial plan 29; strategic description for proposed business practice 29

capital gains tax (CGT) 83

cash 84

cashflow forecast 84

CDM Regulations *see* Construction Design and Management (CDM) Regulations

Certificate of Lawfulness 168

Certificate of Making Good 209

Certificate of Practical Completion 154–155

change control process 206

Change Request format 149, *150*

charitable incorporated organisation (CIO) 22

Charities Act (2011) 23

charity 22–23, 38

chasing payment 95

Cinema 4D 225

client briefing 122–123

client meeting 119–120

client relationship management (CRM) 228

client stage agreements 140

cloud storage 218

CMap 227

The Code for Sustainable Homes 105

collateral warranty 118

commence legal proceedings 95

communication: environmental policy 100; project 119, 121–122

Community Infrastructure Levy (CIL)
168–169
community interest company (CIC)
22, 37
Companies Act 35
Companies (Audit, Investigations
and Community Enterprise) Act
2005 22
Companies House 34, 83, 86;
documentation 35–36
company-wide meetings 72
competence requirements 184
competitions, design 55
competitive tendering 92
Completion Certificate 156
computer-aided design (CAD) 222,
226
computing systems 217; business
continuation 219–220; data
backups 218; hardware
217–218; security 219; storage
and backup 218
concept design plan, RIBA stage
138–140, *139*
conferences 51–52
conservation areas 173
Constructing Excellence 6
Constructing the Team 5
construction contract: management
201–209; tendering timing
of 129
construction cost, percentage of
87–88
Construction Design and
Management (CDM) Regulations
7, 183, 185–186
construction health and safety
185–186

construction industry 5; Building
Safety Act (2022) 10–11;
Construction Design and
Management (CDM) Regulations
7; design-and-build (D&B) 12;
diversity of 11–12; Egan's report
6; Grenfell Tower tragedy 8;
Hackitt's report 8–9; Latham's
report 5; modern methods of
construction (MMC) 7; Morrell's
report 10; trends 12–13
construction management 192–193
Construction Phase Plan 186
Construction Products Regulation 10
construction quality: stages of 147
construction sign-offs 154–155
construction tension 202
construction work: categories of 179
contingency 203
Continuing Professional
Development (CPD) 15, 18, 71
contract administration (CA) 148,
202; management of changes
149
contract form 198–201, **199–200**
contractor drawings review
149–151
contractor's proposals (CPs) 189
contracts 187, *187*; bespoke 115;
categories 187–188; cost, quality
and time 195–198, **197–198**;
design-and-build 189–192,
190, 196; employment 63–65;
management contracts *192*,
192–194, *194*; procurement
arrangement 195; traditional
188–189; type 195–198,
197–198

Control of Substances Hazardous to
  Health (COSHH) 101
co-operatives 22, 38
corporation tax 83, 84
costs 53; fixed *vs.* variable 77
critical path 130

data backups 218
Data Protection Act (2018) 49
Defective Premises Act (1972) 158
defective work 153–154
defects liability period 156–157
deliverables list 123, **124**
Deltek 227, 228
demolition 164
Department for Business and
  Trade 47
design-and-build (D&B) contract 12,
  149, 189–190, 196; advantages
  191; contractual relationships
  in *190*; disadvantages 191;
  variation 190
design-build-and-finance 129,
  190–191
design-build-finance-and-operate
  190–191
design process 90
design responsibility matrix (DRM)
  125, **125–126**
design submission/competition 57
diversity and inclusion 61
dividends 83
domain name 48–49
dutyholders for construction
  183–184

educational buildings 178
efficient project delivery 44

Egan, J. 6, 195; report 5, 6
Employee Benefit Trust 21
Employee Ownership Trust (EOT) 21
employer's liability insurance 40
employer's requirements (ERs)
  189–191
employment: basis of 63; contract
  63–65; non-UK nationals 65;
  specification 61–62
end-of-project appraisal 158
England, planning in 162–170;
  application process 165–169;
  Approved Documents for
  176–177; enterprise zones 164;
  Lawful Development Certificate
  170; Local Plan 162–163;
  non-material amendment
  170; permission required for
  demolition 164; permitted
  development 163–164; use class
  165–169
English Approved Documents 184,
  185
Enscape 225
Environmental Impact Assessment
  (EIA) 167
environmental sustainability:
  Building Research Establishment
  Environmental Assessment
  Method (BREEAM) 101–103,
  102; communications 100;
  Leadership in Energy and
  Environmental Design (LEED)
  103–104, **104**; Passivhaus
  104–105; policy 99–100; of
  projects 101–105; purpose
  of 99; rating schemes 104;
  sustainable office 100–101

exhibitions 51
extensions of time 207

feasibility study 133–135
feasibility study plan 133–135, *134*
Fédération Internationale des Ingénieurs-Conseils (FIDIC) 201
Fees Bureau 87, 92
fees, calculation of 86–87, 96, **97**; competitive tendering 92; fixed sum fee 89–92, **93**; percentage of construction cost 87–88; time charge 89, **90**
fee submission 57
Final Certificate 207–209
Final Payment 207–208
Finance Act (2014) 21
financial management 75–76, **80–81**; income 76; outgoings 76, 77–78; overheads 77–78; practice 76–86; profit 78–79; profit rates 78; tax 79–83
Fire and Emergency File (FEF) 9
fire safety: Grenfell Tower tragedy 8; requirements 13
Fire Safety Information 157
Fire Safety Statement 167
fixed sum fee 89–92, **93**

General Conference of Architects 16
General Data Protection Regulation (GDPR) 49
General Permitted Development Order (1995) 163, 164
Google Analytics 49
Government Construction Strategy 222
Green Business Certification 103

Grenfell Tower tragedy 8
Guide to Safety at Sports Grounds 178

Hackitt, D. J. 8–10
handover process, RIBA stage 154; construction sign-off 154–155; defects liability period 156–157; end-of-project appraisal 158; records 157–158; regulatory sign-off 156
hardware, computer 217–218
headhunting service 61
Health and Safety at Work Act (1974) 65–66
Health and Safety Executive (HSE) 185
Health and Safety File 157, 186
Higher Risk Buildings (HRBs) 10, 11, 182–184
hiring, staff 60–61
His Majesty's Revenue and Customs (HMRC) 31, 33, 41, 78, 79, 82, 83, 94
historic buildings 172–173
hosting, web site 48
Housing Act (2004) 156
HRBs *see* Higher Risk Buildings (HRBs)
human resources (HR) 228–229

identity 46
income 76
income tax 82–83
inflation 94
Information Commissioner's Office (ICO) 49
Instagram 50
Institute of Architects (Scotland) 16

Institute of British Architects 16
Instructions, SBC 2016 204–205
insurance 19, 38–40, 66; *see also*
    employer's liability insurance;
    professional indemnity insurance
    (PII); public liability insurance
intellectual property 64
interim payments 207–208
International Co-operative Alliance
    (ICA) 22
International Passive House
    Association (iPHA) 104
interview process 58, 62–63
invoice 94–95

Joint Contracts Tribunal (JCT)
    198; contract forms 198–201,
    199–200; Standard Building
    Contract (*see* Standard Building
    Contract 2016 (SBC 2016))

Kaye, B. 15
key performance indicators (KPIs) 85

large commercial buildings 44–45;
    vs. smaller project 45
Latham, M. 5, 195
Lawful Development Certificate 170
lead consultant/designer 117
leadership 70–72
Leadership in Energy and
    Environmental Design (LEED)
    103–104, **104**
LEED *see* Leadership in Energy
    Environmental Design
legal site constraints 136–137
legal structure: limited liability
    partnership (LLP) 34; partnership

32–33; private limited liability
    company 35–36; public limited
    company (PLC) 37; sole trader 31
levels of detail (LOD), building
    information modelling (BIM)
    223–224
liability: limited liability partnership
    (LLP) 34; partnership 33; private
    limited liability company 36; sole
    trader 31
Licensing Act (2003) 156
Licensing of Houses in Multiple
    Occupation (Prescribed
    Description) (England) Order
    2018 156
limited liability company 20, 21, 35;
    see also private limited liability
    company
limited liability partnership (LLP) 20,
    33–34
LinkedIn 50
Liquidated and Ascertained
    Damages 207
Listed Building Heritage Partnership
    Agreement 173
local authority: building regulations
    team 120; determination
    168; planning 136, 162–163;
    publicity 167
Local Development Framework 163
Local Plan 162–163
London Building Acts 179
Lumion 225
lump-sum contract form 203–204

management accounts 84
management contracts 192;
    construction management

192, 192–193; management contracting 193–194, *194*
Manufacture and Storage of Explosives Regulations (2005) 178
marketing 43; costs 53; photography 52; planning 45, 46–47, 53–54; purpose of 46
marketing collateral 50–51
material alteration 180
material operation 169
measurement contract 203–204
meetings 45, 71, 101, 129, 220; with authority building regulations team 120; client meeting 119–120; company-wide meetings 72; local residents' 120; pre-application meeting 166; project team meeting 120; shareholders' meeting 36
Microsoft Project 130, 228
model articles for companies 35
modern methods of construction (MMC) 7
monthly reports 85
Morrell, P. 6, 10
multi-disciplinary team (MDT) 183

National Audit Office (NAO) 7
National Building Specification (NBS) 145, 147
National Health Service (NHS) 178
National Heritage List for England 172
National Planning Framework 170
National Planning Policy Framework (NPPF) 161, 162
net contribution clause 118

networking 45
New Engineering Contract (NEC) 201, 207
Non-Completion Certificate 208
non-government organisations (NGOs) 21
non-material amendment 170
Northern Ireland: approval process in 185; building standards application in 185; planning in 171–172
Northern Irish Government website 172
Nuclear Installations Act (1965) 178

Office Manual 212–213, **213–215**
Office of the Scottish Charity Regulator 23
Office Quality Manual 212–213
ongoing project cost control 96–98
Oracle Primavera P6 126, 130, 228
outgoings 76, 77–78
overheads 78; classification 77; fixed *vs.* variable 77–78; rate of 77; on staff costs 89, **90**

partnership 5, 20, 32–33, 84; agreement 32–33; legal structure 32–33; liability 33; tax 33
Partnership Act 1890 32
Passivhaus scheme 104–105
pay as you earn (PAYE) scheme 82–83
payment: chasing 95; interim 207; rates 203
pay-when-paid 96, 118
Pensions Act (2008) 66
people management 59–60, 67–70

percentage of construction cost 75, 86–88
permitted development: Article 4 Direction 164; demolition 164; Prior Approval 164; rights restrictions 164; types of 163
personal contacts 45, 61
photography 52
plan, do, check, act process 212, **212**
plan, do, review, adjust process 70, 129
plan, do, review, update process 53
planning 90, 161–162; application process 165–169; in England 162–170; historic buildings 172–173; law and policy guidance issue 161; in Northern Ireland 171–172; permission 161; principle of 162; in Scotland 170–171; in Wales 171
Planning Act (2008) 162
Planning (Scotland) Act 2019 170
Planning (Wales) Act 2015 171
Planning and Compulsory Purchase Act (2004) 162
Planning Appeals Commission 172
Planning Portal 165, 167
post-completion review 159
Practical Completion Certificate 208–209
pre-application meeting 166
pre-conditions, for new practice 27, 28
press coverage 52–53
Principal Contractor 185–186
Principal Designer 117, 185, 186
Prior Approval 164

private finance initiative (PFI) 192
private limited companies 20, 37, 83
private limited liability company 34–36; legal structure 35–36; liability 36; tax 36
production systems 220–221; building information modelling (BIM) 221–225; virtual reality (VR) 226; visualisation software 225–226
profession: architectural 15–23; Kaye's definition 15; public's trust in 15–16
professional indemnity insurance (PII) 19, 38–39, 115
profit 78–79; rates 78; on staff costs 89, **90**
programming/scheduling software 228
project communications 119, 121–122
project costs 77; plan 131
project enquiry 54–56
project execution plan (PEP) 137, 138, 215
project finances 86–92
project lead/manager 117
project management software 227
project meetings 120; client 119–120; local authority building regulations team 120; local residents/stakeholders 120; project team 120
project programme 126–128, *127*; monitoring 129–130
project team meeting 120
promotion, of the practice 43
provisional sum 203

public consultation 167
publicity 167
public liability insurance 40
public limited company (PLC) 20, 36–37
Publicly Available Specification (PAS) 222

quality assurance (QA) 211–212; core of 212; Office Manual 212–213, **213–215**; Office Quality Manual 212–213; plan, do, check, act process 212, **212**; quality management systems (QMS) 215–216
quality management systems (QMS) 215–216

records: to issue to client 157; to keep in house 157–158
recruitment agency 60–61
Rectification Period 209
Regulatory Reform (Fire Safety) Order 2005 177
regulatory sign-offs 156
Relevant Events 206, 207
reporting, financial 85; annual 86; monthly 85
reputation 46
retirement 65
Rhinoceros (Rhino) 225
RIBA Plan of Work 109–113, *110,* **114,** 121, 129; concept design (stage 2) 138–140, *139*; handover (stage 6) 154–158; manufacturing and construction (stage 5) 148–154, *150*; preparation and briefing (stage 1) 132–138; spatial coordination (stage 3) 140–144, *141*; strategic definition (stage 0) 131–132; technical design (stage 4) 144–148, *146*; use (stage 7) 158–159
Royal Incorporation of Architects in Scotland (RIAS) 16
The Royal Institute of British Architects (RIBA) 15, 16–18; RIBA Chartered Practices 99, 215; RIBA Code of Professional Conduct 59, 113; RIBA Good Practice Guide 87; RIBA mandatory minimum fees scale 87; RIBA Professional Services Contract 113; RIBA Quality Management Toolkit 216; RIBA Standard Professional Services Contract 117, 152; staffing plan for **69**
Royal Institute of the Architects of Ireland (RIAI) 16
Royal Society of Ulster Architects (RSUA) 16

scheduling software 228
Scotland: approval process in 184; building standards application in 184; planning in 170–171
Scottish Building Contracts Committee (SBCC) 198
Scottish Building Regulations 184
Scottish charitable incorporated organisation (SCIO) 22
search engine optimisation (SEO) 49
Secretary of State 169, 180
security software 219

share-related schemes 72
sign-offs: construction 154–155;
    regulatory 156
Simplified Planning Zones 164
site information 135–137
site inspections 151; records 153;
    role 152–153; three levels of
    151–152
SketchUp 225
small detached buildings 179
snags 155
social media 50
sole trader 19, 31, 84
solicitors 27
spatial coordination phase, RIBA
    stage 140–142, *141*; value
    engineering 142–144
specialist employment advice 72
specification 105, 145–148, 153,
    222; employment specification
    61–62
Sports Grounds Safety Act (1975)
    156
Sports Grounds Safety Authority 178
staff handbook 66–67
Standard Building Contract 2016
    (SBC 2016) 117, 154, 157, 201,
    202; adjustment of completion
    date 206–207; clauses 2.26 to
    2.29 206–207; clauses 2.30 to
    2.39 208–209; clauses 3.10 to
    3.22 204–205; clauses 4.8 to
    4.15 207–208; clauses 5.1 to
    5.10 205; completion 208–209;
    Instructions 204–205; Variations
    205
starting an architectural practice 27;
    business plan 28–30; financial

    management 41; insurance
    38–40; name 40–41; pre-
    conditions 27, 28; structure
    31–40
start-up office requirement 229
storage and backup 218
Strategic Forum for Construction 6
sub-consultants 96, 118
sub-contractors 149, 151, 188, 192
successful project outcomes 45–46
Supplementary Planning Documents
    163
sustainability, environmental *see*
    environmental sustainability
sustainable office 100–101

tax 79–83; dividends 83; on fees
    charged 79, 82; limited liability
    partnership (LLP) 34; partnership
    33; private limited liability
    company 36; profits 83; salaries
    82–83; sole trader 31; *see also*
    corporation tax; income tax;
    pay as you earn (PAYE) scheme;
    value-added tax (VAT)
technical design plan, RIBA stage
    144–148, *146*
temporary buildings 179
tender process 90; construction
    contract 129; design-build-and-
    finance 129
termination, contract 117–118
thought leadership 51
time charge fees 89, **90**
Timesheet Portal 227
timesheets 227; client relationship
    management (CRM) 228;
    human resources (HR) 228–229;

programming/scheduling software 228; and project management software 227

Town and Country Planning Act (1947 and 1990) 162, 164, 169

Town and Country Planning (Scotland) Act 1997 170

Town and Country Planning (Environmental Impact Assessment) Regulations 2017 167

traditional contracts 148, 188; advantages 188; disadvantages 189

Twitter (X) 50

uninterruptable power supply (UPS) 220

unitary authority 162

unsolicited enquiries 60, 61

Urban Development Areas 164

Urban Enterprise Zones 164

use classes 165, 170

US Green Building Council 103

value-added tax (VAT) 41, 79–82, **80–81**, 92–95

value engineering 142–144

Variations, SBC 2016 205

virtual reality (VR) 226

visualisation software 225–226, 229

V-Ray 225

Wales, planning in 171

website 47–48; analytics 49; elements of 47; hosting 48; optimisation 49

well-managed projects 70

Welsh Government website 171

winning a project: enquiries 54–56

workers' co-operative 22

written submission 56–58

For Product Safety Concerns and Information please contact our EU
representative GPSR@taylorandfrancis.com Taylor & Francis Verlag GmbH,
Kaufingerstraße 24, 80331 München, Germany

Batch number: 08133665

Printed by Printforce, the Netherlands